Acres of
DIAMONDS
The Russell Conwell Story

GREGORY A. DIXON

With Russell Conwell's Famous Lecture
ACRES OF DIAMONDS

Executive Books
206 West Allen Street
Mechanicsburg, PA 17055
www.ExecutiveBooks.com

TABLE OF CONTENTS

ACKNOWLEDGEMENTS

T he publisher is very grateful not only for the various resources that were available for our use in researching the life of Russell Conwell, but especially for the two authorized biographies of the life of Conwell that were written during his lifetime. These biographies provided the benefit of firsthand quotations from Conwell and from many of his contemporaries who knew him best. Thanks in large part to these resources, our goal to paint an accurate and clear picture of the real Russell Conwell, the great humanitarian, has been accomplished.

The two authorized biographies that were the most useful in helping to write this account—and from which the majority of the quotes that are used in this book were taken—are:

> *Russell H. Conwell And His Work* by Agnes Rush Burr, originally published by The John C. Winston Company Publishers, Philadelphia, PA, 1926
>
> *Acres of Diamonds* by Russell H. Conwell, *His Life And Achievements* by Robert Shackleton, originally published by Harper & Brothers Publishers, New York and London, 1915

The "Acres of Diamonds" lecture that begins in part two of this book was originally printed in *Acres of Diamonds* by Russell H. Conwell, Harper & Brothers Publishers, 1915.

About the Contributors

Gregory A. Dixon wrote chapters one through twelve for the biographical section of this book. He is an entrepreneurial author and media consultant who has performed a broad range of activities related to publishing, broadcasting, and other forms of mass media. He recently assisted in the writing of books for boxing greats Marvis and Joe Frazier and future NFL Hall of Famer Reggie White. He presently resides and works in Harrisburg, Pennsylvania, and he also conducts seminars related to the various books he has written.

Russell H. Conwell (1843–1925), the founder of Temple University in Philadelphia, Pennsylvania, is the author of the "Acres of Diamonds" lecture found at the end of this book. Conwell was described by the great John Wanamaker as "a student, schoolmaster, lawyer, preacher, organizer, thinker and writer, lecturer, educator, diplomat, and leader of men." Besides founding Temple University, Conwell was the pastor of Baptist Temple, one of the largest Protestant churches in America during his day, and he also founded a hospital in the "City of Brotherly Love." His famous "Acres of Diamonds" lecture helped countless individuals to come into the knowledge of the meaning of true wealth and how to attain it without getting sidetracked by selfishness and greed.

INTRODUCTION
AMERICA'S BEST-KEPT SECRET

Located on Broad Street in North Philadelphia, Pennsylvania, and surrounded by many of Temple University's buildings, the illustrious Grace Baptist Church, or "The Temple," where Russell Herman Conwell pastored is presently unoccupied, but it is still standing as a monument to the life and work of a great man. Just the fact that such a large number of students of all races, creeds, and social and economic backgrounds come from all over the nation and the world to attend Temple University—the institution that Conwell founded—in one of the roughest inner-city areas in the country, the very fact that the university still thrives today in a very unlikely place, is a testament to Conwell and his world-famous "Acres of Diamonds" message.

It is surprising, however, that there are many students who graduate from Temple without ever having heard of the school's illustrious founder. And, many individuals who do know of Conwell only know him as the originator of the "Acres of Diamonds" lecture. Most don't realize that Conwell was also the founder of Temple University and the Good Samaritan Hospital (now Temple University Hospital), one of America's first and foremost motivational speakers, and an enormously successful pastor who could be considered the father of the "mega-church" in America. And these are just a few items on his long list of accomplishments! Although millions of people have benefited from Conwell's "Acres of Diamonds" lecture over the decades, there are still countless millions who have yet to discover the priceless nuggets of truth to be found in the rest of his amazing story. Russell Conwell is one of American history's best-kept secrets.

When I first discovered Conwell's story, I felt a deep sense of inspiration as I stood outside of Temple University's McGonigle Hall and looked across the street at the structure of the historical church he established. For years I had driven right by the church and never noticed that it was there. It was like finding acres of diamonds in my own backyard in the North Philadelphia section of the city where I once resided.

This book is about a man who changed millions of lives during his lifetime and is still changing countless lives today with the tremendous legacy that he left behind. Contained in Conwell's life story are priceless lessons about selfless giving and sacrificial living for the benefit of others, and any individual, no matter what race, color, or creed, can benefit from these lessons. It is my sincere desire that this book will serve as a tool to help resurrect many of the noble principles that Conwell practiced and to expose Conwell's great legacy to countless others who need to improve their lives by discovering the "acres of diamonds" right in their own backyards.

Gregory A. Dixon

1
WHO WAS RUSSELL CONWELL?

THE EARLY YEARS OF THE BOY WONDER

Who was Russell Conwell? That question is very difficult to answer in a mere sentence or two. Conwell's amazing list of achievements is so lengthy that it is hard to believe that they were all accomplished in one lifetime. He was a Civil War hero, a graduate of Yale, a high-powered lawyer who oversaw a large practice, the greatest lecturer and motivational speaker of his time, a publisher, an educator, a writer-biographer, a real estate developer, an entrepreneur, a philanthropist who gave away millions of dollars, the pastor of the largest Protestant church in America during his time, the founder of the Good Samaritan Hospital, and the founder of Temple University.

In order to fully understand Conwell's life, we must go back to the very beginning, when he was a poor kid born on a farm in the highlands of Hampshire County, Massachusetts, in 1843. The Conwell family often struggled to pay the mortgage for their humble farm, and they were no strangers to self-denial, hard labor, and poverty, but Conwell felt that those experiences served to develop his character and gave him his greatest education in the university of life.

His father, Martin, and his mother, Miranda, were both caring and compassionate Christians. Conwell grew up during the days of slavery in the United States, and he saw his father constantly putting his life on the line to help fugitive slaves escape to Canada. Though he faced certain imprisonment if he were caught, Martin never allowed the risk to deter him. Conwell once shared with biographer Agnes Rush Burr how he spent many days in dreadful fear because of the great risks his father took:

> During the first ten years of my childhood the little loft over the old woodshed on our farm was very frequently occupied by an escaped slave. Whenever we saw the woodshed locked with a padlock, we knew that a slave was on the inside and that father carried the key. It was not often that we were permitted to see the runaway, as he or she usually arrived at night and was taken away by father during the night. The persistence of those years of gloom have remained with me throughout life; for it was a great and dark secret for the children to keep, and we only mentioned it to each other in very low whispers. But it filled our dreams at night and spoiled

our luncheon at noon in the schoolhouse, and gave us hours of anxious watching for father's return from Springfield.

The line of the so-called "Underground Railway," organized for the assistance of escaping slaves, ran from Virginia through Philadelphia, New York, Springfield (Massachusetts), Bellows Falls and St. Albans (Vermont), and my father had charge of the line between Springfield and Bellows Falls. It was a great sacrifice for him to give the large amount of time and money which he used in helping the colored people to the freedom of Canada, for he never received a dollar or its equivalent in return for his years of labor and expense.

Conwell felt that in spite of his family's struggles and financial lack, his parents set a great example for him to follow and established a wonderful and harmonious atmosphere in their home. He recalled times when he and his siblings played with crude, homemade toys but were still much more cheerful and much happier than many wealthy families who lived in homes with luxurious items.

When, in spite of his poverty, young Conwell was fortunate enough to attend the Wilbraham Academy, a college preparatory school in Wilbraham, Massachusetts, he was so fascinated with the school's library that he couldn't stay away from it and was constantly borrowing books. He kept fifteen to twenty books in his room at one time, and every spare moment he had was devoted to reading them.

In addition to his time spent reading, Conwell joined the debate team at Wilbraham because of his great love for public speaking and debate. His first attempt at giving a speech at the academy in 1857 was a flop because he relied too much on intense preparation and failed to be the natural speaker that God had gifted him to be. He practiced so much that it seemed impossible for him to make a mistake, but, after saying only a few words, he buckled under the pressure and rushed off of the platform. After he recovered from this mildly traumatic experience and redeemed himself at a speech he gave with no preparation at a funeral, he discovered that his greatest strength as a speaker was in being natural and spontaneous. He told Burr:

> Hence, in my life's work, I have never written a lecture or a sermon and have dictated my books. And while I can see that I have often made failures which cause me to blush after many years, yet, with my native eccentricity, I could have done nothing if I had attempted to read my addresses. I most decidedly approve of writing out addresses and sermons and have listened to many a reader with deep fascination. But, for myself, I have been unable to accomplish anything further, or more polished, than in doing my best in what is called extemporaneous speech.

At Wilbraham, young Conwell was determined and willing to do whatever was necessary to complete his education. He and his brother Charles, who also attended the school, worked long hours in order to help pay their way through school. During times when they were penniless, they sometimes went weeks eating only cornmeal mush. They endured great struggles and sometimes even embarrassment because their clothes were homemade and raggedy compared to the finer clothes that many of the other students could afford to wear. They also found it challenging to find time to study and do their homework because they spent so much time working. In spite of their struggles, however, Conwell kept a cheerful and positive attitude and was well-liked among the teachers and students at the school.

As a teenager in 1859, Conwell earned money to pay for his prep school education by selling copies of the biography of the great abolitionist John Brown, a book written and published by James Redpath shortly after Brown's execution. The ambitious teen also obtained permission from the Massachusetts school district to travel around and speak to the school children about the life of John Brown. This marked the beginning of Conwell's first organized series of public lectures. In his later years, he humorously made mention of the fact that those speeches he gave about Brown "must have been a ridiculous exhibition of 'Boy Oratory,' but it did sell the book."

Conwell knew that he wanted to further his education by going to college when he finished prep school, and he learned from many of his teachers and classmates at Wilbraham that Yale was a university that was friendly to the poor and would even help poor students with their work after school hours. Conwell thought he would fit in well at such an institution, so Yale became his number-one choice and eventually his new alma mater. His financial struggles continued while he was at Yale. He worked several jobs to help fund his college education, and he even worked one job at the New Haven Hotel where he received only left-over food for his pay.

Conwell was a lot less outgoing at Yale than he had been in prep school because most of the students at Yale were of an even higher social status than the students at Wilbraham had been. They came from families with money, and Conwell came from poverty. This caused Conwell to stay isolated in his own world, feeling alienated and humiliated. His shabby clothes stood out even more at Yale, and he could not fit in with the average Yale socialite. But one good thing did come out of Conwell's isolation and loneliness: It gave him a greater focus on his studies than many of the other students had.

College life also caused Conwell to begin to view religion differently. He observed that many of the students who had no faith in God had much more, materially speaking, than his family had ever had. Suddenly, the faith of his mother and father began to seem irrelevant and impractical to Conwell. He began to grow bitter and cynical as he noticed the huge gap between the rich and the poor. Furthermore, his memories of church were filled with times when his parents had punished him if he did not stay awake in church. Since he felt that his parents' religion had provided nothing but punishment and poverty, Conwell came to the conclusion that he would no longer believe in God. He became an atheist and an agnostic and actually dedicated some of his efforts toward studying the Bible in an attempt to prove that God did not exist. He took such a firm stance that many of the students around the Yale campus recognized him as an atheist.

Later in life, after he had turned to God, Conwell pointed out that the negative experiences that caused him to deny the faith of his parents actually gave him a greater sensitivity in dealing with individuals who struggled with issues of faith as he had. His experience in searching for the truth put something in him that caused him to be more conscious about making his faith relevant and practical to everyday life—something he felt he was lacking during his childhood years.

When the Civil War broke out, Conwell was eager to enlist because he wanted to stand for justice just like his father did. He never forgot the many fugitive slaves his father had hidden on their very own farm, so to Conwell, the Civil War was about the type of liberty and justice that his father stood for with great courage and conviction. Likewise, Conwell wanted to fight in order to help the slaves go free.

In 1860, shortly before he enlisted, Conwell witnessed a rousing message from Henry Ward Beecher in a Brooklyn church. In the middle of his sermon, Beecher gave an object lesson in which he pretended he was auctioning off a woman—selling her as if she were a piece of cattle. It got his point across, and he then called a young black boy up to the platform. "Sam, come here," he called. When the little black boy had come onto the stage, trembling in fear, Beecher continued speaking to his captive audience with great conviction. He explained that the boy was owned in South Carolina and had run away. Sam's master had offered Beecher an opportunity to purchase the boy's freedom for $770, so Beecher made an appeal to the congregation for the money and ended up getting over $1,700 in the offering plates—much more than was needed. It was a scene that Conwell would never forget, and the visual picture of the selling of humans as if they were mere cattle caused him to better understand his father's sacrifices and see the need to fight in the Civil War in order to help abolish slavery.

The night after Beecher gave his compelling message, Conwell and his colleagues went to a political rally of sorts where they heard a speech by a rather tall, rangy individual who was running for President of the United States. When William Cullen Bryant, a neighbor and friend to the Conwell family, came forward to introduce the presidential candidate, it seemed that very few people in the audience knew the man who would indeed become the next President of the United States. Conwell did not know the man and was not impressed at all with his unusual physical appearance, but the man named Abraham Lincoln spoke some stirring words that Conwell would never forget. He quoted Frederick Douglass' words, "It is written on the sky of America that the slaves shall some day be free," and the audience responded with tremendous applause.

It was not long after that stirring event that Conwell temporarily put his educational pursuits aside in order to enlist in the service. Though he cherished education, he felt a greater urgency to serve his country at that time. He used his eloquence to persuade others to enlist as well, and he became in great demand as a recruiter. Crowds flocked to hear his eloquent speeches that drew large enlistments. His father-in-law, Elizur Hayden, once wrote about how the men flocked to enlist after hearing young Conwell's compelling speeches, and he also mentioned how the ladies fell in love with Conwell and showered bouquets all around him when he came forth with his presentations. He was a popular patriot.

Looking back at those years, a much more seasoned Conwell sometimes wondered why he did not allow all of the fanfare to go completely to his head and cause him to self-destruct with pride. He reasoned that perhaps it was his haunting fear of failure and his fear of audiences as a youngster that helped to keep him in a humble state of mind.

When President Lincoln called for 100,000 men to go to war in 1862, Conwell was one of the first to respond and, at only nineteen years old, he was unanimously elected as captain of his company. The company became known as the "Mountain Boys," and the men had total confidence in Conwell's leadership. When a banquet was organized for the "Mountain Boys" before they went to camp at Springfield, Massachusetts, Conwell was given a sword with the following inscription: "Presented to Captain Russell H. Conwell by the Soldiers of Company F, Massachusetts Volunteer Militia, known as the 'Mountain Boys.' *Vera Amicitia est sempiterna* (True Friendship is eternal)."

Even as a very young leader, Conwell showed signs of selflessness and often made great sacrifices for his soldiers. He met their needs by giving his own pay to soldiers who had no money to buy medicine or by giving his coat to another soldier who was sick and needed it. He led his men with a leadership style birthed out of a simple desire to serve others, and though he was not a professed Christian at the time, his servant spirit caused him to be exalted among his soldiers, demonstrating the Scripture that says, "But he that is greatest among you shall be your servant" (Matthew 23:11).

During the war, Conwell wrote home to tell his family about the sad tragedies of men he had personally seen lose their lives or their limbs. But in the midst of the dangerous battles, he would not desert any of his men who were wounded and in trouble. Because he could not stand to see any of them left to die before his very eyes, he would risk his own life to carry them to safety.

Even when Conwell drilled his soldiers, he led them by example. He put himself wholeheartedly into the work to the point that his soldiers gladly did what he told them to do. Duties that were considered a drudgery with other offi-cers seemed to be much more pleasurable with Conwell. And, though he kept his men working, he was also wise enough to give speeches and organize shows, "sings," or other amusing activities that kept his men from getting too homesick or too depressed about the war.

Tall in stature, with broad shoulders and dark hair, the young Russell Conwell was the epitome of a man's man—and men indeed looked up to him with great admiration. Biographer Robert Shackleton pointed out that after the Civil War, "his soldiers came home with tales of his devotion to them, and of how he shared his rations and his blankets and bravely risked his life; of how he crept off into a swamp, at imminent peril, to rescue one of his men lost or mired there." As a young soldier in the Civil War, Conwell was already beginning to show the traits of a great leader who would eventually influence an entire generation of people.

2
RUSSELL CONWELL'S PERSONAL ENCOUNTERS WITH HISTORY-MAKERS

JOHN BROWN, FREDERICK DOUGLASS, WILLIAM CULLEN BRYANT, ABRAHAM LINCOLN, AND OTHERS

Conwell's father, Martin, was a man whose life was often filled with extraordinary escapades. He bravely met with many distinguished and radical individuals at the Conwells' little hillside farmhouse to discuss plans to violate unjust laws in order to help acquire freedom and justice for black slaves. The Conwell house was also a stop on the Underground Railroad, and Conwell's father drove across the country with hidden slaves. After the slaves were taken from Philadelphia, Pennsylvania, to New Haven and then on to Springfield, Massachusetts, Conwell's father would meet them and continue with them on the route to Bellows Falls and Canada. "Those were heroic days," Conwell remembered. "And once in a while my father let me go with him. They were wonderful night drives—the cowering slaves, the darkness of the road, the caution and the silence and dread of it all."

As a kid, Conwell saw John Brown, the radical abolitionist, for the very first time in 1852. Brown's giant, hairy presence frightened young Conwell at first, but he and his brother began to see Brown in their home so often that they naturally grew to love him very deeply, and he became known to them as "Uncle Brown." Uncle Brown always slept in the northwest bedroom when he visited, and one of Conwell's fondest memories of Brown was seeing him patiently train one of their old horses to walk home from the schoolhouse all alone.

Brown had an office in Springfield, Massachusetts, and Martin Conwell was essentially in a sort of partnership with him. Brown, a white revolutionary with a hatred for injustice, believed that he was ordained by God to put his very life on the line in order to help free the black race from enslavement.

On October 16, 1859, with a party of twenty-one, which included his sons and five blacks, Brown invaded the state of Virginia, captured the town of Harpers Ferry, seized the United States armory, and freed fifty slaves. Initially, Brown and his men did not attempt any type of offensive action, occupying only defensive positions in the town, but when they were surrounded by the local militia and the

United States marines under the command of Colonel Robert E. Lee, ten of Brown's men (including two of his sons) were killed in battle. Brown was wounded and forced to surrender; he was then arrested and charged with treason and murder, along with other crimes. Martin Conwell tried to sell his house to get some money to help with Brown's defense, but he was unable to do so, and Brown's execution went forward.

Before hearing his sentence, Brown was allowed to address the court. He said:

> I believe to have interfered as I have done, . . . in behalf of His despised poor, was not wrong, but right. Now, if it be deemed necessary that I should forfeit my life for the furtherance of the ends of justice, and mingle my blood further with the blood of my children, and with the blood of millions in this slave country whose rights are disregarded by wicked, cruel, and unjust enactments, I submit: so let it be done.

It was a sad day for many free and enslaved blacks when they knelt and wept in honor of Brown as his body hung from the gallows in Charleston, Virginia, in December 1859. When Frederick Douglass paid his last respects to Brown, he made the following statement: "Brown's struggle in the cause of freedom was superior to mine. Mine was a small light; his was a burning sun. Mine was bound by time; his stretched away to the silent shores of eternity. As a black man, I am willing to speak for the slave; John Brown, a white man, was willing to die for the slave. How do you explain this?"

Russell Conwell explained to biographer Agnes Rush Burr the agony that his family experienced over Brown's hanging:

> Well do I recall December 9th, of 1859—the day on which John Brown was hanged. Only a few weeks before he had come to our house and my father had subscribed to the purchase of rifles to aid in the attempt to raise an insurrection among the slaves. The last time I saw John Brown he was in the wagon with my father. Father gave him the reins and came back as though he had forgotten something. John Brown said, "Boys, stay at home! Stay at home! Now, remember, you may never see me again," and then in a lower voice, "And I do not think you will ever see me again. But remember the advice of your Uncle Brown" (as we called him), "and stay at home with the old folks, and remember that you will be more blessed here than anywhere else on earth. The happiest place on earth for me is still my old home in Litchfield, Connecticut."
>
> On the 9th of December, 1859, which was the day set for the execution of John Brown at Winchester, Virginia, my father called his family into the kitchen at eleven o'clock and commanded that all should remain quiet without speaking a word until the clock struck twelve. He took down the old Bible from the mantel and seemed to make an effort to read in the Psalms; but he did not read aloud and his tears must have soon blotted out

his view of the words.

My father had received, only two days before, a letter from John Brown, which he had written in jail and in which he sent his love to the boys, asking them to think of him sometimes in after life as one who had humbly tried to do his duty. That bell emphasized all his goodness of heart and repeated his good deeds of kindness to us as children; and while we felt that he was extreme and somewhat fanatical in his declarations and plans, yet we knew full well that his heart was set on the service of God and his intention was noble and pure.

In our home on the day John Brown was hung there was a funeral of the sincerest kind. We children ate but little and our parents did not taste of food, I do not recall ever having heard my father weep aloud at any other time, as he did when the clock struck twelve on that awful day.

That experience filled us with extreme prejudices against the people of the South and, from that day until the slaves were emancipated by Abraham Lincoln, our souls were filled with bitterness and hatred, which are the usual accompaniments of war. And it has taken more than half a century for all the people on both sides to see how useless and fratricidal, after all, that war was. How much better it would have been to have accepted President Lincoln's recommendation and purchased the slaves of the South at their normal valuation and set them free without revolution and without bloodshed.

Brown's radical exploits seemed shocking at first, but many Northerners eventually began to speak positively about the militant abolitionist. "He did not recognize unjust human laws, but resisted them as he was bid," said Henry David Thoreau in an address to the citizens of Concord, Massachusetts. "No man in America has ever stood up so persistently and effectively for the dignity of human nature."

"With this series of revolutionary acts, the white militant almost single-handedly created the passionate emotional climate that led to the Civil War," stated Dr. Claud Anderson, author of *Dirty Little Secrets*. "More than any other white before or since, Brown confronted the issue of black liberation forthrightly at a high personal cost. He sacrificed not just his own life, but the lives of a number of his own children."

Many of the abolitionists of his day regarded Brown as a courageous martyr for the cause of human freedom. Whether or not historians agree with Brown's militant revolutionary methods, no one can doubt that his uncompromising commitment to equality for blacks was not just mere rhetoric. John Brown was serious about his mission.

John Brown was not the only world changer and history maker that Conwell had the privilege of knowing. He also had a personal encounter at his home with Frederick Douglass, the great orator. During this encounter, Conwell's father introduced Douglass by saying, "Boys, this is Frederick Douglass, the great colored orator."

Young Conwell looked at Douglass and said, "He isn't black. He is white."

"Yes, boys, I am a colored man," Douglass responded. He went on to explain that his father was white and his mother was black. "I never saw my father and I remember little of my mother except that once she tried to keep an overseer from whipping me, and the lash cut across her own face, and her blood fell over me."

That story was one that Conwell and his family never forgot. Douglass came to the Conwell home many times more after that first encounter, and Conwell remembered him as a tireless worker who devoted his life to the freedom of his people.

William Cullen Bryant was a neighbor to the Conwell family, and he also joined with them in the fight against the unjust institution of slavery. Conwell once told Burr of Bryant's influence on his life:

> I have never forgotten the advice he gave me one day … for when I told him that I was not able to earn sufficient money to go away to school, he told me that many of the greatest men in America had not been able to go to school at all, but had learned to study at home, and had used their spare hours with books which they carried about in their pockets. After that, for more than thirty years I carried various books and learned seven different languages, using the hours of travel, or when waiting at stations, in reading and careful study. It always surprises a young man to find how much he can learn if he used his spare hours with some book which he has conveniently placed in his pocket. By far the greatest part of my useful education was obtained in such circumstances.

In addition to meeting history-making men like Brown, Douglass, and Bryant, Conwell personally met with President Abraham Lincoln during the Civil War. Over the course of his life, he also met in the homes and wrote about the lives of just about every man who became president after Lincoln.

The personal encounters that Conwell had with men like John Brown, Frederick Douglass, and William Cullen Bryant helped to shape his character in later years. And, the passion to help the oppressed that he saw in his mother and father undoubtedly left an indelible imprint on Conwell's impressionable young mind. It was an imprint that would later inspire him to provide millions of dollars of his personal income to aid the underprivileged.

3
WHY RUSSELL CONWELL VOWED TO DO THE WORK OF TWO MEN

THE TREMENDOUS TALE OF JOHN RING

This intriguing story begins when Conwell was a soldier in the Civil War. After his term of enlistment with the "Mountain Boys" of Company F ended, Conwell was asked to do some more recruiting and head up another division. Company D, the Second Massachusetts Regiment of Heavy Artillery, was formed, and Conwell was again made captain.

It was also at this time that a young lad by the name of John Ring became an orderly and Conwell's personal assistant. Ring, a sixteen-year-old who looked up to Conwell as a hero, practically begged to work at Conwell's side. Conwell was reluctant to grant Ring's request, because he did not want the boy to be exposed to the dangers of war, but the lad and his father were so insistent that Conwell eventually gave in.

John Ring became like Conwell's shadow. He loved and respected his captain, was always at his side, and obeyed his every command. One particular night, however, when Ring was doing his evening Scripture reading, Conwell, who was an atheist at the time, began to mock Ring and told him to never read the Bible again. Although Ring respected Conwell to the utmost, he had a greater love and reverence for the God of his Bible, and from that point on he left Conwell's tent to read his Bible. It was the only time he disobeyed Conwell.

Ring was saddened by the fact that the man he admired so much did not believe in God, but he still continued to serve Conwell with complete loyalty in spite of their religious differences. They shared the same tent, and Ring was constantly at the captain's side to wait on him or nurse him when he was sick. Ring also vowed to protect and cherish the sword that had been given to his captain by the Mountain Boys.

The courageous Captain Conwell did face numerous life-threatening experiences while he was out fighting in the war. In one instance, he had a shootout with a Confederate soldier and was shot in the shoulder. The Confederate soldier, who was a bit more experienced than Conwell, saved his last bullet until

Conwell's ammunition was all used up. Then he ran from behind a large pine tree and shot Conwell. Fortunately, Conwell's men were able to capture the Confederate, and Conwell's wound did not seem very serious at the time. The brass bullet was not removed from his shoulder, however, and the brass corroded and ate into his lungs, years later causing hemorrhages that almost ended his life.

It was also years later when Conwell met up with and befriended the Confederate soldier who had almost killed him. Conwell remarked, "It goes to show how war will inflame men's hearts with the spirit of murder, even when there is no basic reason for it. If men were not stirred up by spasmodic eruptions of hate for each other, the sense of brotherhood would quickly develop. It is in most men waiting to be developed."

On another occasion, when Conwell and his men visited a farmhouse to get horse feed, the Southerners received his army in a hospitable manner. They later sent some persimmon beer to the camp for Conwell to drink, and he gladly received it. Their earlier show of hospitality, however, had been mere trickery, intended to deceive Conwell into drinking the beer, which had been secretly poisoned. The beer made Conwell seriously ill and kept him bedridden for weeks. In fact, it took years for his system to become totally free of the poison and the damaging effects it had on his body. While Conwell was still recovering, the faithful and dedicated John Ring cared for the captain and never left his side.

After Conwell had recovered enough to leave his bed, he went on a special journey to Newbern to resolve a situation that was hindering his men from getting their pay. He did not realize that he would later be penalized for being absent because he had not gotten an official leave of absence. While he was away, he heard the horrible news that the Confederates had defeated some of his men at Newport. Conwell immediately tried to return to Newport to see about his men, but he could not get to them because the countryside was filled with enemy troops and the woods were on fire. Having no other choice, Conwell gave up his quest and returned to Newbern, only to hear more crushing news: His beloved orderly, John Ring, had been killed while attempting to save Conwell's sword from the Confederates.

The tragic event had taken place one day when the Confederates attacked Conwell's soldiers near Newbern. Conwell's soldiers escaped across the river and set the bridge on fire after crossing it so that the Confederates could not pass over. Without anyone noticing it, the undersized John Ring slipped past the Confederates to rush back into Conwell's tent and grab the sword off of the tent pole where it was hanging. After seizing the sword that was so precious to him, he dodged the enemy troops and dashed for the bridge just as it was starting to catch on fire. As he tried to cross over to the other side, the smoke and flames grew more intense. Ring crawled and staggered, leaning over the edge of the bridge to catch his breath and get fresh air.

THE RUSSELL CONWELL STORY

Soldiers from both sides witnessed Ring's losing effort to make it across the bridge. Suddenly, an honorable Confederate officer felt sorry for the kid and commanded everyone to cease firing by waving his white handkerchief. "Tell the boy to come back here and we will let him go free!" the Confederate yelled.

Unfortunately, Ring could not hear the yelling from either side due to the noise and intensity of the flames. For a few brief moments every soldier went totally silent as Ring temporarily disappeared from view inside a covered part of the bridge. They had begun to lose all hope for him when suddenly Ring came out of the flames and made it to the other side of the bridge. At his sudden reappearance, soldiers from both armies gave an enormous yell. But Ring's clothes were blazing with fire, and he fell into the water. His soldiers quickly dragged him out of the water and rushed him to the hospital in an unconscious state.

Conwell later got the report that John Ring had stayed unconscious in the hospital for a day or so before he finally came to himself and noticed that the sword that he had saved was right beside him. It brought a smile to his face, and he took the sword in his arms, hugged it to his chest, gave a few final words to the soldiers to pass on to Conwell, and then slipped into eternity. Conwell's men told him how Ring's burned body had fallen into their arms, and they also told the captain of Ring's last words in the hospital: "Tell the Captain I saved his sword."

The horrifying news of his orderly's tragic death, as well as all of the other traumatic experiences Conwell had gone through were more than he could bear. The most wonderful boy he had ever known, John Ring, was dead—dead because he had risked his life trying to honor his hero. The captain was overwhelmed with deep anguish and shock at the devastating report. He was so overtaken that fever attacked his body and he tossed in frenzy for days. His fever grew worse when he got word that he would be unjustly court-martialed for being absent without leave while his men lost the battle.

As time went on, Conwell eventually recovered and resolved the issue related to the court-martial, and he was eventually given a higher position as a lieutenant-colonel in General James B. McPherson's army. While fighting with the army at Kenesaw Mountain, Georgia, Conwell was severely wounded and left to die.

There is something about a near-death encounter that will make a man wonder about the true meaning and purpose of life, and so was the case with Russell Conwell. As he lay all night among dead bodies and dying men, he faced the grim reality that there was a great likelihood that he would also be dead before the morning.

Reality took a brighter turn, however, when Conwell was rescued the next day by a search committee that had been assigned to find his body because he was an officer. Conwell was grateful to be alive as he was taken to the Big Shanty

Hospital near Marietta, Georgia, but he agonized more than ever over the fact that he did not know the real meaning and purpose of life. Undoubtedly, he was reminded of the way his faithful Christian friend John Ring had lived and died. The young colonel began to think more seriously about the faith of his mother and father, and he suddenly found that he needed answers about eternal matters because he had come face to face with the reality of how quickly death could come.

Conwell was at a key turning point in his life, a point at which he needed a real solution that would satisfy his thirsty soul. He knew he could no longer be satisfied without getting reassurance regarding his spiritual condition. He sent for the chaplain and asked him some questions that had been troubling his mind in a very deep way. The questions related to whether or not there was an afterlife and whether or not friends would meet again in the other world and know each other. Of a certainty, Conwell wanted to see John Ring again in the future.

After discussing these issues with the chaplain, the matters regarding eternal life became clearer for Conwell. He humbled himself under the mighty hand of the Lord and accepted Christ as his Savior, and he was never the same again.

Conwell was once asked if that experience was what he would consider his conversion experience. He answered,

> Yes, except that I would say decision must go with conversion. It is not only a matter of emotion. One must do something. Merely getting excited and doing nothing is not conversion. Decision and action must go with the change of thought, or else it is not real. It is only effervescence. True conversion changes the main purpose of life from selfishness to unselfishness; from the desire to have one's own way to a willingness to do whatever God commands, no matter what the consequences.

As soon as Conwell was discharged from the hospital, he publicly professed his new faith, and from that point on, his relationship with Jesus Christ and the principles he applied from the Holy Bible gave him a firm foundation for everything he attempted or accomplished in life.

His desire to honor John Ring's sacrifice motivated him to make a special vow. Conwell told one of his biographers:

> When I stood beside the body of John Ring and realized that he had died for love of me, I made a vow that has formed my life. I vowed that from that moment I would live not only my own life, but that I would also live the life of John Ring. And from that moment I have worked sixteen hours every day—eight for John Ring's work and eight hours for my own.
>
> Every morning when I rise I look at this sword, or if I am away from home I think of the sword, and vow anew that another day shall see sixteen hours of work from me.
>
> It was through John Ring and his giving his life through devotion to me that I became a Christian. This did not come about immediately, but it came before the war was over, and it came through faithful Johnnie Ring.

THE RUSSELL CONWELL STORY

In later years, Conwell reminded himself of John Ring's great sacrifice by hanging the sword over his bed in his Philadelphia home. He vividly remembered the undersized sixteen-year-old boy who had been devoted to him to the point of sacrificing his very life during the Civil War. Whenever Conwell visited his hometown in the Berkshires where he and Ring were both from, there was also another vivid reminder of the sacrifice Ring had made: In a little cemetery in the Berkshires, a few miles from Conwell's old home, there was a plain stone that marked the resting place of little Johnny Ring.

4
RUSSELL CONWELL THE LAWYER, WRITER, AND ENTREPRENEUR

After the Civil War ended, Conwell completed law school at Albany University in New York and was admitted to the bar. In 1865 he married Miss Jennie Hayden from Chicopee Falls. With a new wife came added financial responsibilities, and Conwell had to do whatever it took to make ends meet before his law career became profitable. He was a humble man who did not let pride get in his way, and he relocated to Minnesota and took jobs that required him to saw wood, plant potatoes, or perform other menial tasks in order to take care of his responsibilities and finance his vision.

Conwell's new wife was ambitious, sweet, loving, and committed to helping him with his life's endeavors. She was a dedicated wife who always encouraged him and stuck with him in spite of their humble beginnings. Conwell adored her, confided in her, and talked things over with her. Together they were willing to pay whatever price was necessary to accomplish their goals for the glory and honor of God.

Due to his great determination and strong work ethic, it did not take long for Conwell to improve his financial conditions. He worked as a writer for the St. Paul Press, and at the same time he began to practice law and also went into the real estate business. He supplemented his income even further by giving singing and piano lessons in his law office. Outside of work, Conwell spent much of his time sharing Christ with others. He also started a choral quartet in which his wife sang soprano and he sang bass.

Based on a need in the marketplace, Conwell helped to start a daily newspaper called the *Minneapolis Daily Chronicle,* as well as a weekly publication called *Conwell's Star of the North.* From the very beginning, Conwell made it clear to his readership that the paper was not owned or controlled by any organization or political party and that his primary goal was to stand for justice and speak the truth. "We will try to the best of our ability to carry into the family with the *Star* a high standard of morality, a love for the good, a respect for the noble, and an increased interest in education, refinement, and everything that elevates and dignifies mankind," he wrote in his editorial in the first issue.

Jennie, who wrote editorials for the newspaper's "Ladies' Department," was ahead of her time in the progressive stances that she took regarding equality for women. During a time when many men wanted to limit or diminish the abilities of women, Jennie made it clear that the "Ladies' Department" of that newspaper would reflect the fact that women were interested in more than just cooking or fashions. She also made it very clear that she believed that the woman was mentally man's equal. Elaborating on this point, she wrote, "Whatever she has done, in nearly every instance, has been appropriated and claimed by men. Who supposed, until very recently, that the mowing machine—the greatest improvement of the age—a machine that saves our farmers hundreds and thousands of dollars every year—was the invention of a woman?"

A bold yet very balanced editorialist, she also pointed out that the woman's "place is not man's place; that her physical and mental constitution is different from man's and calls for different exercises; that there is enough for both to do in the world and neither need to be termed 'inferior.'" She further stated that the newspaper did not adopt the extreme stance that some of the radical feminists of their day took, but neither did their paper support "the other extreme which would treat women as an 'inferior order of animals.'"

Without a doubt, Russell and Jennie Conwell were a progressive husband-and-wife team that made unique contributions to their city. In his law office, Conwell held a noon prayer meeting every day for a year, and some of the attendees of the meetings were so inspired that they branched out with Conwell to help start the YMCA of Minneapolis.

In 1868, a calamity occurred when Conwell's house caught on fire on a very cold winter night while he was not at home. Every thing was lost in the fire, and around the same time Conwell was also stricken with a mysterious illness that caused hemorrhages and much blood loss. His finances dried up because he was not able to conduct any of his business in Minnesota, so he decided to move back east.

The condition of his health was so serious that it was speculated that he only had a few weeks to live, but Conwell refused to give up hope, and his doctor eventually discovered that his mysterious illness was actually caused by the brass from the bullet that Conwell had been struck with while fighting in the war years earlier. An operation was performed, the bullet was removed successfully, and Conwell's health was miraculously restored.

Because they had lost practically all that they had, he and his wife went to Boston in 1870 and started over again. They were extremely grateful for the second chance that the Lord had given them. They were poor, but they were very happy and always exemplified an attitude of gratitude, knowing that God was able to fully restore them. It was also a happy time because their first child, Nima, was born.

THE RUSSELL CONWELL STORY

The Conwells began to see an improvement in their circumstances as Russell worked for the *Boston Traveller*, opened a law office, began to lecture, and started traveling around the world as a newspaper correspondent. In his travels he conducted interviews with many famous individuals, including an interview with Charles Dickens just a few days before the famous writer died.

In addition to writing many books on a variety of general topics, Conwell also wrote biographical books on U.S. Grant, Rutherford B. Hayes, John Wanamaker, James A. Garfield, and others. Because he had met and interviewed Charles Spurgeon, a publisher asked Conwell to write Spurgeon's biography shortly after the prolific theologian died. Conwell wrote the *Life of Charles H. Spurgeon* in only two weeks by dictating the book to his secretary while he traveled on the train during the day. The book became a bestseller and sold 125,000 copies in only 4 months. Conwell did not keep any of the royalties but donated them to a mission. He was eighty years old when he wrote the *Life of John Wanamaker*. Although it was difficult for Conwell to find the time, he wrote the biography of Philadelphia's millionaire merchant prince because Wanamaker had requested him to do so.

Though Conwell became recognized as a prolific, best-selling author in his day, he was never interested in pursuing a writing career, and during those days he was better known as a lecturer. Editors and publishers from all over the country approached him to work on various projects, but he often turned down many of these opportunities because of his focus in other areas.

In addition to writing a number of books, Conwell also loved to read books for his personal enrichment and development. He especially loved to read biographies or books on other topics related to real-life events. He eventually accumulated a very extensive library in his Philadelphia home; it included hundreds of books about theology, poetry, biblical history, character-building, and more.

While he was still in Massachusetts, and as his law practice grew, Conwell decided to do something that no other law firm or attorney had done in the history of Boston: He offered legal services to the poor, free of charge. Like a champion to the oppressed, Conwell prevented numerous poor people from being ripped off or taken advantage of by dishonest wealthy people. As the following notice he placed in a Boston paper indicated, Conwell never took a cent for the legal services he provided:

> Any deserving, poor person wishing legal advice or assistance will be given the same free of charge, any evening except Sunday, at No. 10 Rialto Building, Devonshire Street. None of these cases will be taken into court for pay.

It was not uncommon for Conwell to have fifty people a night in his law firm in response to his ad. Conwell also provided free legal services to many of the widows and orphans of soldiers who needed help to get their pensions. He never gave up on a case regardless of its difficulty. His partners also reported that he never lost a pension case—and never made a dime from any of the cases, either.

Russell Conwell was also a man of great integrity. He purposed in his heart that he would never represent individuals if he knew that they were crooked or guilty. Because he had such a great compassion for the downtrodden, however, some deceitful individuals tried to take advantage of his kind and caring nature. Conwell was once tricked into representing a pickpocket who was accused of stealing a watch from a man. After the compassionate attorney got the pickpocket acquitted of the charges, the pickpocket ended up paying Conwell with money he had stolen from Conwell's very own wallet while in the courtroom! Fortunately, the pickpocket was ashamed and confessed to Conwell. He actually decided to go straight and also asked Conwell to take the watch and return it to the man it had been stolen from.

Conwell's compassionate attitude also caused him to take drunkards into his home and care for them throughout the night. When the morning came he would implore them to change their lifestyles. At times he also demonstrated his compassion toward others by acting as a guardian to numerous orphan children.

A Bible study he started while living in Boston further proved that Conwell was a resourceful man of great compassion and powerful influence. He was recognized by one observer as a man who did not influence others to get caught up into "the petty religious prejudices of the day." At the time Conwell was a lay leader in the Tremont Temple Baptist Church in the Boston area, and he started a Bible class that rapidly grew to a congregation of more than 2,000 people. He would give a talk in reference to the Sunday school lesson and then follow with a question-and-answer session. His format was so practical, lively, and relevant to everyday problems that thousands of businessmen from the Boston area were attracted to the meetings. Conwell also mobilized various members of his class to apply the biblical truths they learned in the class to real-life situations by going into the slums of Boston to do community service.

Conwell's second child, Leon, was born during these years, and Conwell continued to serve his community while he also cherished and provided for his family. The well-rounded community servant also continued to work as a lecturer, writer, and lawyer, had a successful real estate operation, and participated in political, religious, and community affairs.

In the midst of his good fortune, great tragedy came suddenly and without warning when in 1872 Jennie passed away after being sick for a few days. The days following the devastating death of his beloved wife were indeed dark days for Conwell, and to keep his mind off of the tragedy, he worked nonstop and even taught himself five foreign languages while he traveled back and fourth to work on the train. The tragic event caused Conwell to become even more serious about eternal matters, starting him on a greater quest for a deeper depth in his faith.

In due time Conwell opened up his heart to the possibility of marrying again. While sacrificing his time to study the Bible and reach out to the less fortunate, his ministry activities allowed him to cross paths with Miss Sarah Sanborn. Though Sanborn came from a wealthy and influential family, Conwell was impressed by the fact that she had an unselfish heart that caused her to reach out to the less fortunate. She was also a well-rounded woman with exceptional intellectual and business skills, and she was actively involved in various ministry activities. Their common interests sparked a mutual attraction between the two, and they eventually were married in 1874.

As Conwell and his new wife spent more and more time around their colleagues in the ministry, Conwell began to get a clearer vision of his purpose. He made a major decision at the age of thirty-seven to shut down his law office and real estate business, answer the call to the ministry, and become a preacher for a small Baptist church with only a handful of members in Lexington, Massachusetts. It was a radical decision that marked the beginning of an entire new season in his life.

5

BUILDING THE LARGEST PROTESTANT CHURCH IN AMERICA WITH ONLY FIFTY-SEVEN CENTS

C onwell's first involvement in the ministry was with the church in Lexington, Massachusetts, and this involvement came about because a woman asked him for some legal advice regarding whether or not to sell the little, broken-down church. Conwell set up a meeting and advised the handful of members to go on with running the church rather than to sell it. When one member voiced the opinion that the building was too broken-down to use, Conwell agreed and offered to work with the people to fix it up.

Though the people seemed encouraged by the idea, nobody but Conwell showed up to work the next day. The average man would have been discouraged under those circumstances, but Conwell was the type of motivator who was known for his ability to convince even the most doubtful or weak individuals to cooperate with a plan. After coming to the conclusion that it would be better to build a new church than to try to patch things up, Conwell took hold of his ax and started tearing down the dilapidated old building by himself.

A man who wasn't even a church member asked Conwell why he was tearing the building down and eventually offered $100 toward the building of a new church. Another man came by and saw the commotion and offered a $100 donation as well. In due time, the church members were convinced that Conwell was serious, so they also chipped in with their labor and their money.

Since the church no longer had a minister, Conwell ran back and forth from Boston to preach for them in a rented room. At that time he was still working in his law practice and was not even an ordained minister; he was simply filling a need. "And it was there in Lexington, in 1879, that I determined to become a minister," he told biographer Robert Shackleton. "I had a good law practice, but I determined to give it up. For many years I had felt more or less of a call to the ministry, and here at length was the definite time to begin. Week by week I preached there and after a while the church was completed, and in that very church I was ordained a minister."

Some of his friends and relatives—and even some of the church members—felt that his decision to enter the ministry was a quick and extremely foolish choice that would lead to poverty and failure. But Conwell was convinced and satisfied that he was going in the right direction according to the will of the Lord. Years after entering the ministry, he explained to biographer Agnes Rush Burr how he felt before and after his dramatic decision: "Before that, I was always changing. I was restless. Though I was busy; though I was what the world would call successful, I wasn't satisfied. From the moment I decided on this work, I was contented and happy. I felt a great satisfaction that cannot be described in words."

Conwell also admitted that he should have gone into the ministry sooner but had fought against it because of a lot of misconceptions he had developed about ministry and church as a child. Because of his negative childhood experiences with the church, he had not been able to see any connection between ministry and purposeful living. After answering the call, however, he felt that he had a new-found mission to help others find their ultimate purpose in life.

Although he faced much criticism and ridicule for taking the risk to enter the ministry, Conwell later testified to Burr:

> I surrendered all and kept on amid the scoffs and reproaches of my best friends. And while I have seen hours of trials; met sore defeats; been wounded by jealousies; injured by misunderstandings; yet, as I look back upon life now, I cannot see that I ever suffered greater hardships than I expected. Instead of those expected privations, I have been especially blessed. The Lord has sent to me successes beyond my highest expectations, and I have had friends and comforts which I am sure I could not have deserved. … Defeats are often the greatest victories; and the Lord may use most those who seem to be—from a human point of view—of the least account.

After Conwell preached his first service in the small Lexington church, the second service was filled to capacity, with an overflow of people standing on the outside as well. Conwell's practical teaching and preaching ignited the town and made a tremendous impact on the townspeople's quality of life in general. Although Conwell was focusing primarily on ministry at that time, he did not toss his business skills to the side. He used his keen business sense to help develop Lexington from a commercial standpoint, and the small town began to flourish with new opportunities.

From Lexington to the Philadelphia Pastorate

Conwell spent only eighteen months at the ministry in Lexington, during which time he helped to raise thousands of dollars to complete the new church building. Just as the church in Lexington was flourishing and Conwell was gaining more and more influence in the community, he was called upon to help save a dying church in Philadelphia. The church that desperately wanted his services, Grace Baptist Church, had an unfinished building and was tied up in debt and about to go under. When Conwell visited Philadelphia in order to survey the community and decide whether or not he would make the move, he was deeply touched by the members of the little struggling church who hungered for change, and he also felt that Philadelphia needed him more than Lexington.

He made the decision to go to the "City of Brotherly Love," and once again his friends and family members felt that he was making a foolish mistake. How could he leave a flourishing church that he had worked so hard to establish to take on a project with a dying church? It seemed illogical, but Conwell was the type of man who only wanted to be where he felt the Lord was calling him at the time.

Obviously, his congregation in Lexington did not want to see him go, but they supported him nonetheless. It was a sad day in Lexington when he gave his farewell message, but the people agreed that Conwell had equipped them to carry on the work that he had begun, and they also accepted the fact that the Philadelphia congregation needed him more than they did.

Immediately after relocating to Philadelphia, Conwell began to preach and organize the people to accomplish their goals. He was an innovative leader who was not bound to following traditions that were of no practical use to the people. Individuals who visited the church were very impressed with the warm and friendly atmosphere and the way the congregation gave Conwell their undivided attention when he began to speak. One visitor even commented that he had never been in a church where he felt so warm and welcome; he said that the church was not stiff or restraining like so many other churches. The ushers were also known to be extremely polite, and all the church members were taught to make visitors feel right at home as well.

The simplicity of the service, the clear reading of the hymns, the richness of the praises unto God, and the short and concise nature of the prayers left a very positive impression on the visitors. Some first-time visitors were also surprised to see that the offerings were painlessly expeditious, without any pulling or begging whatsoever. The giving was totally voluntary and willful. It was not a church service steeped in vain tradition.

One particular individual who had heard some strange and negative things about the church before visiting for the first time was pleasantly surprised at the uplifting nature of the service and determined that the criticism was probably motivated by envy or jealousy. The church service was jam-packed, with people standing in the aisles. In a simple yet forceful and conversational way, Conwell preached his spontaneous sermon to the congregation without the least bit of form or fashion. It was obvious that he understood the common people and did nothing for vainglory but was merely interested in helping his congregation to learn and apply relevant truths.

In spite of his wonderful accomplishments, Conwell was often criticized and misunderstood, although many of the people who criticized him for being over-ly sensational or outlandish were only going by hearsay and had never been to any of the church services. His church was referred to by some as "Conwell's Folly." Conwell once told Burr how he reacted when he was criticized or misun-derstood by others: "I do not do reckless things. That would be wrong. But when I think I am doing right, I go ahead, and let people say what they will. I take my stand."

If Conwell was guilty of anything, it was simply of doing things differently from most other churches. He was more focused on doing things out of a sincere sense of purpose than out of vain religion or meaningless tradition, and he had a reputation of being different from the average minister.

John Wanamaker, the Philadelphia businessman who had great respect for Conwell, once shared how many ministers had basically "prophesied" Conwell's failure because they did not think that his unorthodox methods would be fruitful. At a celebration in honor of Conwell's seventieth birthday, Wanamaker shared how one particular minister who at first did not trust Conwell eventually experi-enced a change of heart after Conwell reached out to him while he was sick:

> But one day he was very ill, and a beautiful white azalea came to his bed-side. At first he almost resented it. Why did that man send him a flower? What motive was back of it? Did he intend to buy him with a present? Well, he wasn't to be bought—that was all! Nevertheless he would watch him, and watch him he did. He began to see the motive of a great Christ-like life, of which that white flower was just one expression. He found Russell Conwell doing little kindnesses here and there—to high and low alike. He found a great, wide, deep interest in humanity for Christ's sake such as he had found in no other life, such as he presently longed for in his own. And upon the day of that man's funeral, Doctor Conwell said, "I feel personally bereaved, for in my Philadelphia ministry he was one of my earliest, dearest, and most sympathetic friends."
>
> The same distrust to which this brother freely confessed personally, existed in larger circles also—just because he was "different." When he read that Jesus went about, "preaching, teaching and healing." Doctor Conwell said, "That is the model for every organized Christian institution; preaching is not enough; there must be added teaching the ignorant and healing the sick." Hence the night school which has grown into the Temple University, and the Samaritan Hospital—and later the adoption of the Garretson Hospital.

As Wanamaker had indicated, Conwell was indeed a man of high character. He was also a tireless worker who had a down-to-earth and approachable nature. Under his direction, the seating capacity of the Philadelphia church was increased to 1,200, and in less than a year there was standing room only. Tickets had to be issued to members free of charge so that they could be admitted through the back door before the large crowd of strangers and visitors was allowed to enter. Unfortunately, certain individuals in the city used this to criticize the church by claiming that one had to have a ticket to get in and also claiming that the tickets were for sale. However, no one was excluded from entering the church through the front door if he cared to wait amidst the crowd. The tickets were only a means to keep order, and they were never offered for sale.

The Little Girl with the Red Pocketbook

Conwell was very disappointed that his church often had to turn away people— even children—who were hungry to attend the services. As the church's membership grew, there arose an obvious need to expand the facilities, and the biggest motivation for the Grace Baptist Church to begin a new building fund had a lot to do with a six-year-old girl named Hattie May Wiatt.

On one particular Sunday morning, little Hattie, along with several other children, was not able to enter Sunday school at Grace Baptist Church because there simply was not enough room for them. Hattie took this much harder than all of the other children and began to shed heartfelt tears.

Conwell recalled seeing the little girl crying, lifting her up on his shoulder, and taking her into the back of the crowded Sunday school room. He also remembered telling her on another occasion that they would one day have a room big enough for everyone so that in the future Hattie and others would not have to be left standing outside.

After she went home that day and pondered the situation, Hattie resolved that she would do something on her own to make it possible for the Grace Baptist Church to expand so that she, along with other children, could have a regular place in the Sunday school. She started saving up all of her pennies in a little red pocketbook so that she could donate the money to help build a larger facility.

Just a few weeks later, however, tragedy struck, and Hattie was suddenly overtaken by a serious illness that took her life. Before she died she told her mother that she wanted the money in her pocketbook to be given to the Grace Baptist Church so that they could build a larger facility. At the precious little girl's funeral, her parents handed Conwell Hattie's savings of fifty-seven cents.

Conwell was very moved. He later shared Hattie's story with his congregation and initiated some creative fundraising ideas based on little Hattie's initial sacrifice in order to expand the Sunday school facility. This motivated the congregation to buy a house north of the church at Berks and Mervine to accommodate more children. When the Sunday school quickly outgrew that facility as well, the congregation started a building project in order to accommodate many more people in the future. The trustees, also inspired by the little girl's sacrifice, made a determination to buy a lot on Broad Street to build the new church facility. When Conwell shared the tale of the fifty-seven cents with the man who owned the lot—a man who wasn't even a churchgoer—the man was immediately stirred and decided to sell the land to the church for a very good price and at a very low mortgage rate. All he wanted for a down payment was the "fifty-something" cents!

Not long after these astonishing events occurred, some members of the congregation surprised Conwell at his house one day, telling him that thousands of dollars had been raised and the land for the church was now totally debt-free.

The ground for the new building was broken in 1889, and in March of 1891 the new church was opened for worship. The sanctuary was arranged with 3,135 chairs, but it actually had a maximum seating capacity of 4,200 if more chairs were needed. Although the actual name of the church was Grace Baptist Church, the new edifice was commonly referred to as the Baptist Temple—or simply "The Temple."

Starting with a mere fifty-seven cents, the Lord had allowed Russell Conwell to build and fill to capacity the largest Protestant church in America at the time. In a sense, one could say that Conwell was the father of the mega-church in America—and it was a little girl's legacy that made all the difference.

6
RUSSELL CONWELL'S KEYS TO SPECTACULAR CHURCH GROWTH

The fact that Russell Conwell experienced spectacular church growth in spite of the poor circumstances of his congregation was certainly no accident. Conwell fully understood that in order for any organization to flourish, its atmosphere must be conducive to growth and productivity. This chapter highlights some of the primary characteristics in Conwell's ministry that made the difference between stagnation and healthy growth. The timeless human relations, spiritual and organizational insights that Conwell employed can be applied to a broad spectrum of circumstances for the purpose of enhancing growth. If properly applied, any leader in any industry or profession can benefit from these concepts.

Unity, Cooperation, and Sacrifice

Russell Conwell and his congregation proved that exercising unity, cooperation, and sacrifice could enable even a group of people with minimal financial resources to overcome obstacles and experience tremendous success. Because Conwell's Philadelphia congregation was basically poor, the process of expanding the facilities of the church proved to be a challenging venture. There was no one in his congregation who had the ability to make large contributions, yet by the grace of God, Conwell and his members built one of the largest and most beautiful edifices in the country.

Many of the people in Conwell's congregation only had enough money to cover their basic living expenses, so they cut back on their costs in order to save and set aside money for the building fund. Other members started walking in order to save their carfare for the fund. Some sacrificed their summer vacations or gave up the bad habit of smoking in order to save money. Boys and girls inspired by little Hattie Wiatt's story also saved their pennies and made contributions.

Surprising sums of money came in as a result of these various efforts, and Conwell trained his workers to be practical and productive in all that they did. A fair was held in Philadelphia that was visited by thousands of people. It was conducted in a very sensible and business-oriented fashion, and it netted about $9,000 for the building fund. That was a lot of money at the time!

Because Conwell's congregation caught hold of his vision, they were motivated to temporarily deny themselves of some of the basic comforts of life for the good of the ministry. They unified and cooperated with one another in a selfless fashion, organizing and working with the fair and other functions on a totally volunteer basis. They were also motivated to sacrifice their time, talent, and treasure for the benefit of the church and the community at large because Conwell helped them to see a vision and a purpose that went beyond their temporary needs or pleasures. His visionary leadership inspired the people to come together with the type of unity, cooperation and sacrifice that brought forth dramatic church growth.

A Focus on Building People More Than Bricks and Mortar

It is important to point out that Conwell never allowed his congregation to lose focus of the need for constant spiritual growth in the midst of all the building and fundraising efforts. Consequently, the church's membership continued to experience numerical growth as well as spiritual growth throughout the building process. Conwell never sacrificed the act of building people for the desire to build an edifice. On the first Sunday in the new building, the *Philadelphia Press* reported that "during the opening exercises, over nine thousand people were present at each service."

The Spirit of Excellence

Although Conwell's congregation primarily consisted of poor people, he taught his congregation that they did not have to remain poor, because there was no lack in God. Years later, while on a trip to London, Conwell recalled his experience as a visitor at a very uncomfortable and shabby church, and he expressed his opinion that the ministry needed to be done in excellence:

> Oh! It is all wrong to make it so unnecessarily hard to listen to the gospel. They ought for Jesus' sake to tear out the old benches and put in comfortable chairs. There was present an air of perfunctoriness and lack of object, which made the service indefinite and aimless. This is a common fault. We lack an object and do not aim at anything special in our services. That, too, is ill wrong. Each hymn, each chapter read, each anthem, each prayer, and each sermon should have a special and appropriate purpose.

Based on his philosophy of excellence in ministry, "The Temple" was carefully constructed with elegance and distinction. The church was extremely large for Conwell's day and time. With a 4,200-person seating capacity in the sanctuary, the church also had a dining room with a seating capacity of 500, Sunday school rooms able to hold 2,000, several business offices, and more. Prominent speakers who came to the church purported that the acoustics in the auditorium were nearly perfect and that no one in the audience ever had to strain to hear the messages. It was a state-of-the-art facility that demonstrated Conwell's ability to accomplish tremendous goals with the highest level of excellence.

Conwell, understanding that in every person there is a natural attraction to the comfortable and the aesthetic, did not underestimate the value of an excellent facility, and his standard of excellence in ministry helped the church to grow because it motivated members to invite friends or family members to visit the church. The spirit of excellence that permeated the church attracted people from all walks of life who wanted to be associated with a church that had the dignity to represent itself in the best possible way.

Understanding the Danger of Success

Conwell was definitely an accomplished pioneer who was ahead of his time, but he was also keenly aware of the pitfalls of success and warned his congregation about this issue in a sermon called "Danger of Success":

> Ah, that is a dangerous hour in the history of men and institutions, when they become too popular; when a good cause becomes too much admired or adored, so that the man, or the institution, or the building, or the organization, receives an idolatrous worship from the community. That is always a dangerous time, and small men always go down, wrecked by such dizzy elevation. Whenever a small man is praised he immediately loses his balance of mind and ascribes to himself the things which others foolishly express in flattery. He esteems himself more than he is and, thinking himself to be something, he is consequently nothing.
>
> How dangerous is that point when a man, or a woman, or an enterprise has become accepted and popular! Then, of all times, should a man or the society be humble. Then, of all times, should they beware. Then, of all times, the hosts of Satan are marshaled to overcome by every possible insidious wile and open warfare. The weakest hour in the history of the greatest enterprises is apt to be when they seem to be—and their projectors think they are—strongest. Take heed lest ye fall in the hour of your strength. The most powerful mill stream drives the wheel most vigorously just before the flood sweeps the mill to wildest destruction.
>
> The mission of the church is to save the souls of men. That is its true mission. It is the only mission of the church. That should be its only thought. The moment any church admits a singer that does not sing to save souls; the moment a church calls a pastor who does not preach to save souls; the moment a church elects a deacon who does not work to save souls; the moment a church gives a supper or an entertainment of any kind not for the purpose of saving souls, it ceases in so much to be a church and to fulfill the magnificent mission God gave it. Every concert, every choir

service, every preaching service, every Lord's Supper, every agency that is used in the church must have the great mission plainly before its eye. We are here to save souls of dying sinners. We are here for no other purpose. And the mission of the church being so clear, that is the only test of a real church.

Conwell knew that a spirit of arrogance, superiority, elitism, or pride detracts from the success of any institution. On the other hand, the ability to keep a level head and remain humble is a quality to be admired in any true leader or institution that has experienced enormous success. The spirit of sincere humility with a focus on the Lord that Conwell instilled in his congregation attracted many more visitors and new members to the church. It was the combination of an understanding of the danger of success and the principle of humility that caused Conwell's church to flourish. "By humility and the fear of the Lord are riches, and honour, and life" (Proverbs 22:4).

Miraculous Transformations

Because Russell Conwell exercised humility, he did not take self-reliance to an unhealthy extreme. He understood the need to rely on God's supernatural power beyond what Conwell was able to do in the natural realm.

Conwell shared with biographer Agnes Rush Burr a miraculous story of how a set number of new converts were inexplicably added to his congregation on a weekly basis:

> I have found many people, however, who yet disbelieve the statement that just seven different people appeared in our congregation every week during five full years and stated their desire to find the Lord. Summer and winter—rain or shine—holidays or workdays—the same number presented themselves without any previous attempt to regulate it, to the continued astonishment of myself and the people. There are hundreds of living witnesses that know such to have been the fact, by having been present through the entire five years. All attempts at an explanation have utterly failed to establish any definite reason for such a condition of affairs.

Because Russell Conwell was a man who possessed supernatural faith, the church also grew in supernatural ways that were not explainable to the natural mind.

A Spirit of Consecration and Reverence in the Church

Conwell's church was known for a consecrated atmosphere in which individuals were not distracted by discord and were instead free to focus on worship. Conwell explained to Burr that his church had a Discipline Committee that was not much needed due to a reverential atmosphere in the church:

I do not recall that in the thirty-three years of my church life in Philadelphia, there has ever been called before the "Discipline Committee" a single member accused of wrongdoing in the church. There must have been evil persons among the thousands who came and went through the membership of the church in those years. But the spirit of worship and sincere consecration was so powerful that such persons either soon left the church or repented and turned into the current with the rest, without friction or scandal.

A good reputation attracts members to an institution and enables it to grow. Because Conwell's church was not plagued by scandals and because so many of the church's members were upstanding examples in the community, the church experienced great success. "A good name is rather to be chosen than great riches, and loving favour rather than silver and gold" (Proverbs 22:1).

A Congregation That Networked and Met Practical Needs

Conwell testified that in a congregation that consisted primarily of common working people, "through twenty-five years, there was not known to be a single member of that church out of work a month who desired a position." The tightly knit nature of the social fabric of the church meant that it was not uncommon for members to help other members get jobs. The members so much sought for opportunities to do good that all needs were met very quickly if a member happened to fall upon hard times.

The *Philadelphia Press* once reported an incident that demonstrated how the men of the Baptist Temple looked out for one another's personal welfare:

> At one time a member of Grace Baptist Church became involved in financial difficulties in a very peculiar way. Previous to connecting himself with the church, he had been engaged in a business which he felt he could not conscientiously continue after his conversion. He therefore sold his interest and engaged in mercantile pursuits with which he was unfamiliar. As a result he became involved and his establishment was in danger of falling into the sheriff's hands.
>
> The situation became known to some members of the Business Men's Union of the church and a committee was appointed to look into his affairs. His books were found to be straight and his stock to be valuable. The members immediately subscribed the thousands of dollars necessary to relieve him of all embarrassment, and the man was saved.

The young women of the church served in a way that benefited members and visitors alike. One of their primary goals was to attract new members, and they also assisted in prayer meetings, developed plans for Christian benevolent work, welcomed young women to the church, visited the sick, engaged in various follow-up activities, held home devotional gatherings, supported missionary work, secured employment for the underprivileged, taught homemaking skills, worked as nurses' aids at the hospital, developed and coordinated various activities and entertainments for youth, acted as "big sisters" to younger girls, and much more.

The young men of the church also served in a similar fashion. In addition to helping to increase membership, they organized young men's Bible classes, selected consecrated leaders for the various leadership positions, directed Sunday morning prayer meetings, invited individuals walking by the church to enter and welcomed strangers, brought back those who wandered astray, established relief committees for lost young men, provided hospitality to traveling businessmen and brought them to the church, promoted self-control and purity, unified with other strong young men and developed plans for reaching men in the streets, shopping areas, offices, schools, colleges, etc., visited the sick, helped the unemployed or underemployed to find gainful employment, and planned social events and fundraising activities.

On certain occasions, members who were willing to give up their seats for standing visitors would inform the ushers in advance. There was always a prevailing attitude in the church that motivated the congregation to meet the practical needs of members and visitors alike.

Conwell understood that where there is a true spirit of caring and sharing, an institution will experience growth. All of the activities and outreaches of his church helped the ministry to grow, because the church developed a reputation as an institution that went beyond mere preaching and actually met the needs of the total person from both a spiritual and a natural standpoint.

Keeping Spiritual Purposes and Priorities Straight

Everything Conwell inspired his congregation to do was driven by purpose. Even if the church sponsored a community fair with all types of entertainments and activities, there was ultimately a spiritual purpose behind the event. For Conwell, the purpose of the "church fair" was evangelical, and everything boiled down to saving souls.

At a typical fair, individuals (even non-Christians) contributed items to sell to raise funds, and there was wholesome entertainment and costumes. The fairs offered a lot of opportunities for the community, were very creative, and were done in excellence. People responded as if they were going to a carnival, and the fairs actually brought a large number of new members to the church and raised money at the same time. There was also a sign-in list so that the church could send a note of appreciation to those who attended. It was Conwell's way of maximizing every opportunity to reach people.

Conwell believed in using entertainment for the purpose of providing wholesome alternatives or drawing people to Christ, but he warned against the vulgar or irreverent amusements of the world. He also warned against entertainment brought into the church just for mere secular purposes or just to make money. The focus, he declared, should always be on the saving of souls, and every tool available should be used without compromise for the purpose of influencing men for good. Every method of entertainment suggested for ministry purposes had to be first brought before the Board of Deacons for a vote so as to keep impure or irreverent activities from entering into the church, and Conwell constantly reminded his congregation that the true mission of the church was "not to entertain people" but to turn their hearts to God.

Spontaneity and Relevance Rather Than Vain Religion

Although Conwell believed in upholding the reverent and purposeful spiritual traditions of the church, he was not stuck on vain traditions or pointless protocols. His congregation was accustomed to his sincere and spontaneous actions. In one particular service, while the congregation was singing, Conwell got out of his seat and knelt down beside it in the pulpit, with his back facing the congregation. He stayed in that position for several minutes while he spontaneously offered reverential prayer or praise to his God—and no one in the congregation seemed to think that it was odd in any way.

In addition to having an atmosphere that was neither stiff nor stifling, the church also sponsored a number of relevant events such as lectures featuring ex-Presidents of the United States, educators, writers, and others. There was an innovative and fresh spirit in the church that went against the grain of vain religion and reached people who typically would not have been interested in coming to church.

The church was sometimes criticized as going too far into the world, but Conwell's mission was to be uncompromising yet practical and relevant to the people who needed the message of the gospel the most. He did not want to have a pious and self-righteous church that was irrelevant and aloof from the thousands of lost souls that needed to be reached. He knew the importance of combining changing methods with unchanging principles.

To Conwell, balance was the key of life. He did not subscribe to pointless, vain religion, and neither did he believe in totally relying on the self-guided efforts of man. Conwell would say that "unless God lives in the house, they labor in vain who build it" (see Psalm 127:1). His church grew because members and visitors alike were in a place that was sometimes unpredictably exciting, relevant, and fresh, unlike some of the other dull religious organizations they had experienced in the past.

Wise Use of the Business-Minded

Conwell ran a very efficient, business-minded operation in order to maximize resources. Money was constantly coming in and going out of the church for the purpose of helping others, and many people marveled at the extraordinary results that the financial organization of the church achieved.

With more than 3,000 members, the church found it necessary to keep and update records, and members had to receive communication and follow-up. To keep the congregation and the community informed of the relevant activities and purposes of the church, the church published a magazine called the *Temple Review.*

Conwell and his staff believed in staying current with the latest technologies and developments of their time, and if a particular system no longer worked in a practical manner, it was tossed aside and changed to something more current and more efficient. The staff realized that what works today might not be relevant for tomorrow, so they were constantly keeping themselves informed of the latest business methods combined with unchanging spiritual principles in order to continue the growth of the church.

Conwell also made it a point to effectively utilize those leaders in his congregation who had a keen business sense. The men who handled the business affairs of the church were men of character, integrity, experience, and action. While some people merely said pious prayers for the lost sheep to come home, these men went out after the lost sheep and brought them home. Conwell expressed the fact that these men were insightful enough to relate to all classes of people and "read men at a glance." These consecrated and competent men were pillars of the church, and it was not easy to pull the wool over their eyes.

The church went to great lengths to get men who were balanced with consecration and competency for their Board of Trustees. Focus was also a key ingredient in the success of the church when it came to handling business and financial affairs. According to the rule of the church, a man could only hold one elective office.

The trustees primarily attended to the financial matters of the church, while the deacons primarily dealt with issues related to the membership. If a member was absent for three consecutive Sundays, the deacons would follow up with him. They were careful to show their care and concern for the membership by either sending letters or through personal visitation from time to time.

From a financial standpoint, Conwell and his astute leaders built a multimillion-dollar ministry with sophisticated checks and balances built into the system. For example, the church treasurer was only at liberty to withdraw funds as directed by the Board of Trustees and certified by the chairman and secretary. During Conwell's pastorate, millions of dollars were raised in support of the church, charitable work, missions, Temple University, and three Philadelphia hospitals (Samaritan, Greatheart, and Garretson).

Conwell once shared with Burr the important roles played by the businessmen in his church:

What has contributed most as a means used of God to bring Grace Church up to its efficiency? It was the inspired, sanctified, common sense of enterprising, careful businessmen. The disciplined judgment; the knowledge of men; and the forethought and skill of those workers who were educated in the school of practical business life helped most. The trustees and working committees in all our undertakings—whether for church, hospitals, university or missions—have been, providentially, men of thorough business training who used their experience and skill for the church with even greater care and perseverance than they would have done in their own affairs. … Some men make religion so dreamy, so unreal, so unnatural, that the more they believe in it the less practical they become.

In order for any institution to experience maximum growth, it is necessary to appoint leaders with a keen business sense along with great organizational skills. Conwell did not diminish the value of people who were educated and trained in business matters, and the church grew all the more as a result of the contributions that were made by these individuals.

Excellence in the Music Ministry of the Church

Music was an important element in the church, and the music programs were also conducted with excellence in order to draw and inspire people. The organ that was used in the church cost $16,000. Other instruments that were utilized to inspire and uplift the service included horns, concert flutes, a clarinet, a trumpet, a xylophone, a bass drum, a snare drum, a triangle, various other percussion instruments, and more.

Conwell, who loved music from his childhood days, played several instruments, had taught music when he was a young man, and sang. The church's director of music, Professor David D. Wood, was a blind organist who organized a 250-voice choir and motivated them to faithfully attend rehearsals and sing together with tremendous harmony. Since most of the choir members were common people who volunteered their musical abilities after working long hours at their regular jobs, this was a commendable task that demonstrated the great leadership ability of the beloved Dr. Wood.

Known all over the country, Wood had a reputation as a master musician who was also responsible for teaching more organists than any other teacher in Philadelphia at that time. He did not expect his singers to be perfectionists but simply required a good voice and a good ear. His goal was to get them to sing well, and he was careful not to overtrain them—especially since many of his singers were "non-professionals." He believed in giving plenty of praise to his singers whenever it was due, and he was opposed to dominating or ridiculing his singers, but he corrected faults promptly and kindly. The choir performed with such excellence that spectators came from near and far to witness them in concert.

Because Wood's hallmark was excellence, he imposed a strict standard on his choir. He maintained that rehearsals, which were not to exceed two hours, must begin promptly and not be interrupted by any type of disorder. When the chorus was first formulated, members actually paid a fine if they missed a rehearsal. In spite of this controversial policy (which was later discontinued), the chorus still flourished, and they cheerfully followed Wood's guidelines because of their love for music and the desire for excellence that was instilled in them by their leader.

Wood was careful not to dictate musical tastes or disregard his choir members. He gave them a variety of music that went beyond the scope of traditional church songs in order to accommodate a variety of interests. He gave choir members opportunities to perform songs of their own choosing so that he would have their full cooperation when it came to performing the songs of his choice. To maintain enthusiasm, he gave his choir something challenging to perform but was always careful not to put too much pressure on them. He was opposed to being timid, however, and made it a point not to be afraid to attempt great things with his choir. The reputation of the choir was so outstanding that they were invited to perform at various high-profile secular functions.

Conwell and Wood both understood that music is a universal language, so they were insightful enough to invest the resources necessary to build an excellent music ministry that would help the church to grow and attract individuals from all walks of life.

Purpose-Driven Church Services That Met Practical Needs

Sunday services at Conwell's church began at 9:30 a.m. with a prayer meeting in the lower part of the church facility. For twenty-one years Conwell was always at prayer at 9:30 a.m. sharp, until his traveling on the lecture circuit prevented him from doing so in later years. After prayer, the service would then cover special topics, focusing on each topic for three months at a time. The regular church service began at 10:30 a.m. in the main sanctuary, and Conwell would cordially greet many of the visitors after the service.

Since Conwell had had many negative experiences as a child forced to sit through adult church services, the church had a separate service (the children's church) specially designed to appeal to young people. Many other churches have utilized this concept over the years since its implementation by Conwell.

The children's church was divided into two separate categories (over and under ten years old), and the carefully selected teachers were required to be smart, attractive, of good character, trained and experienced with modern teaching methods, as well as individuals who loved children and were also loved by children. To make the format more appealing to the youngsters, movies that educated, amused, and edified the children were shown on top-quality equipment that was on the same level as that of any movie theatre of their day.

The children's church was also used as an effective means to reach out to family members of the various children who attended. Each child was given a card to take home to be filled out with the names and birth dates of their fathers and mothers, brothers and sisters, and grandparents. Conwell then personally signed and had birthday cards sent to the various family members. In addition, each year the children's church put on one or two special events to further the growth of the church and to raise funds to help defray the cost of running the ministry.

For the young people who were "neither children nor grown-ups" a special Young People's Vesper Service was held every Sunday night at 7:30 p.m. Different young people took turns leading the service while some played instruments, read Bible verses, etc.

The church also conducted Sunday school classes for various age groups ranging from kindergarten to adult. In the adult class, Conwell devised an innovative format in which he would address issues from "the question-box." This was a very popular feature in which he answered a variety of questions about life or Christian living that were sent by mail or handed to him on the platform. The service was extremely popular and attracted men and women from various parts of the city.

Baptisms were frequent at the church and usually took place on Sunday mornings in a beautiful atmosphere while music was played softly in the background. Since these services represented a new life in Christ, Conwell gave special care to making them memorable events. The fifteen-by-sixty-foot baptismal pool was designed with a beauty matched only by nature itself. All year long, the sides of the pool and pulpit were decorated with beautiful flowers, palms, and vines, with a stunning little waterfall at the back of the pool. It was always a sight to behold when as many as 175 or more children, teenagers, adults, or silver-haired elderly were "buried with Christ by baptism into death to be raised again in the likeness of His resurrection." They were partakers of an event that signified that they were burying their old sinful lives and rising out of the water with a new life in Christ.

Conwell also instituted such unique features as baby dedications and New Year's Eve "watch-meetings" (better known today as "watch-night services"). His New Year's Eve services began with prayer at 8:00 p.m. Around 9:30 p.m., an intermission was held, with light refreshments served by the young people, and the watch-meeting began at 11:00 p.m. and ended at midnight when the New Year began. The one-hour watch-meeting service started with Conwell praying for guidance in the New Year, renewed consecration, and a better Christian life for the church and for individuals. After hymns were sung while the church orchestra played, Conwell would ask members to stand as a symbol of their rededication to the Lord and then invited others to come to God for the first time. At midnight, everyone in the congregation would wish one another a cheerful "Happy New Year" and the informal fellowship would begin as the formal service ended.

The uniqueness and relevance of the church services to the various age groups and categories of people met spiritual needs with a freshness and relevance that captivated the congregation and further stimulated the growth of the church.

Miraculous Prayer Meetings

For Conwell, innovative and organized church services alone were not enough to make the church all that it needed to be. He heavily relied on the power of prayer and thus held a weekly prayer meeting as one of the most important keys to building a healthy church. According to Conwell, his weekly prayer meeting was very popular for three reasons:

1. United prayer
2. Social acquaintances
3. Counsel

An informal, family atmosphere was the hallmark of the prayer meetings at the church. The format, which Conwell said could help the people in any church, consisted of a more open setting that allowed for a free sharing of ideas. Conwell helped to accomplish the goal of creating a family-like atmosphere that made those in attendance feel right at home when he entered the service giving out handshakes and warm greetings.

The meetings would usually open with a short prayer followed by a song. A chapter from the Bible that related to the evening's topic would be read and then was followed by a brief talk. Conwell would then tell the people that the rest of the meeting was in their hands. If necessary, he would calmly provide inconspicuous direction to keep the meeting from growing dull, but this rarely needed to be done. At Conwell's prompting, Scripture verses were shared publicly by dozens of individuals in the span of only a few minutes. Along with breaks for singing and private prayers, testimonies were sometimes shared as the Spirit led. Individuals were also invited to rise to their feet so that Conwell and the church could publicly say a prayer for their direction and strength.

After the services ended, Conwell always instructed a committee or various members of the church to take time to talk to the individuals who requested prayer and also to take their names and addresses. Conwell would later pray personally for each of those individuals and would sometimes even write them letters. It was often that the prayers were miraculously answered in a direct and unmistakable fashion: On one occasion, a dying child was miraculously healed at the very hour that the prayer took place in the church.

The miracle of answered prayer in Conwell's church proved that Christianity was a real faith that actually worked in the lives of the people. This further contributed to the growth of the church and attracted new members as many individuals truly experienced the reality of God's power and presence in a tangible way in the church.

A Committed, Qualified, and Compassionate Leader

Since it has been said that everything rises and falls on leadership, it is important to emphasize that "The Temple" had the ultimate advantage of being under the guidance of a man who had exceptional leadership qualities. Conwell was known as a leader who was extremely efficient at accomplishing tasks and delegating authority to his staff. In a nutshell, he was a tireless worker who also knew how to get work done through others. Though he was extremely well-read and knowledgeable, he was not the egocentric type of leader who had to do it all and know it all. He was wise enough to assign the type of individuals who had the expertise that he lacked and also to give them the authority to do their jobs properly.

His institutions were great because he knew how to choose the right leaders and he also knew how to inspire greatness in his staff. His staff was devoted to him and his ideals, and Conwell was never too busy to see any of them if they needed his help or advice.

One of Conwell's biographers observed that he was so thoroughly systematic with the use of his time that he could attend to intricate details, take necessary time out with staff, and keep several institutions running in a splendid fashion all at the same time. He seemed to be a master at maximizing time and employed several secretaries for different purposes. He often made use of his travel time by dictating to a secretary while on the train.

Conwell also had a secret that helped him to avoid procrastination: his "Do-It-Now" rule. This very simple rule was one of the keys to his ability to accomplish many things at once. Whether a task was small or large, Conwell made up his mind that he would not put it off until the next hour or the next day if it was something that absolutely needed to be done right away. This kept his responsibilities from piling up on him and allowed him to accomplish many things that would not have otherwise been done.

He had the ability to deal with an enormous amount of correspondence while he was involved in several "occupations" and at the same time had to prepare two sermons and two talks every Sunday. He was a compassionate "people person," and at the end of services he typically shook hands with hundreds of parishioners. After a service it was not uncommon for him to say something like, "I shall be here for an hour. We always have a pleasant time together after service. If you are acquainted with me, come up and shake hands. If you are strangers come up and let us make an acquaintance that will last for eternity."

ACRES OF DIAMONDS

It was not difficult for visitors to see why one of the trademarks of the church was the ability to make strangers feel right at home with no pretense. Conwell sincerely loved people, and those who had the opportunity to be in his presence could sense his genuine concern for them. He had a unique ability to make the common man or woman feel ten feet tall. Success had not gone to his head, and from his standpoint, it was always an honor and a privilege for him to be a servant to God's people.

An institution can never rise above the vision or qualifications of its leadership, and Russell Conwell was recognized as a leader among leaders. The maximum growth and productivity of any institution only takes place when followers truly believe in the leader's ability to fulfill the vision at hand. Because Conwell was a caring leader who practiced what he preached and led by example, his staff and congregation had the confidence to eagerly follow him without reservation or hesitation. The keen leadership qualities he possessed were without a doubt one of Russell Conwell's greatest keys to spectacular church growth.

7

HOW RUSSELL CONWELL STARTED TEMPLE UNIVERSITY FROM NOTHING

Contrary to what many might assume, the idea to start Temple University did not come about as the result of any type of planning or forethought. It was started simply because of a youngster who asked a question of a man who did not stop at merely giving a verbal answer.

The youngster who asked the question was Charles M. Davies. The person he asked the question to was Russell Conwell. The conversation took place one evening after a church service when Conwell noticed that Davies, a member of the congregation, seemed very disturbed about something. Conwell, being the perceptive man that he was, knew that the youngster had something heavy on his heart that he wanted to share. So Conwell asked the young man to sit down next to him, knowing that it would be only a mater of moments before Davies would share his troubling thoughts.

"Dr. Conwell," Davies said, "I earn but little money, and I see no immediate chance of earning more. I have to support not only myself, but my mother. It leaves me nothing at all. Yet my longing is to be a minister. It is the one ambition in my life. Is there anything I can do?"

Conwell explained to Davies that any person with determination and ambition could achieve his goals to become a minister by studying at night. The young man, with all sincerity of heart, explained to Conwell that he was ready to give every minute of his spare time in order to accomplish his goal, but he just didn't know how to start.

Davies' sincere desire and determined attitude inspired Conwell right then and there to offer the young man more than mere rhetoric or sympathy. Conwell immediately gave Davies a workable solution: "Come to me one evening a week and I will begin teaching you myself."

Davies, delighted that Conwell was willing to personally take the time to teach him, asked if he could bring a friend with him. Conwell told Davies to bring as many friends as he wanted, and on the first night of personal instruction,

Davies brought six friends with him. By the third evening session, there were forty students in attendance.

As it is so often said, "the rest is history." Other educators eventually volunteered their services to help Conwell teach, a room was rented, and then a couple of houses were rented as well. That handful of students and teachers eventually turned into a college, buildings were erected on Broad Street next to the church, and the college ultimately became a great university. It is not difficult to figure out where the school's name came from, as it was located near Conwell's church, "The Temple." The founding of Temple University, a major institution even today, came about simply because a young man without money asked a question and Conwell wanted to help meet his need.

Knowing that knowledge is wealth and power, Conwell believed that people stayed in poverty mainly because they lacked access to the type of education that could change the mind and the circumstances of the underprivileged. He was troubled by the fact that he could not give "fish" to eat to every poor and hungry person who came to him for help. He realized, however, that he had a much better chance of teaching thousands of poor men and women "how to fish" and feed themselves. In a letter to a family member about how he had developed the idea for Temple University, Conwell wrote:

> It was no new truth; no original invention, but merely a simpler combination of old ideas. There was but one remedy for all of these ills of poor and rich, and that could only be found in a more useful education. Poverty seemed to me to be wholly that of the mind. Want of food, or clothing, or home, or friends, or morals, or religion, seemed to be the lack of right instruction and proper discipline. The truly wise man need not lack the necessities of life; the wisely-educated man or woman will get out of the dirty alley and will not get drunk or go to jail. It seemed to me, then, that the only great charity was in giving instruction.

Consequently, Temple University was birthed out of a deep sense of need and purpose. In a nutshell, Conwell started the university with three primary goals in mind:

1. To give education to those suffering from lack, poverty, and hunger in order to improve their lives

2. To give education to average working-class citizens so that they might increase their earning potential by learning to make more money in less time in order to enjoy the better things in life

3. To give education to those who were already rich in material goods but poor in the knowledge and compassion of serving others so that they might utilize their resources to properly serve others

The number-one reason the university was founded, however, was for the purpose of giving an education to those who were unable to get it through the usual channels. Conwell knew what it was like to be a poor and needy college student, so he had a special compassion and concern for underprivileged individuals who wanted to further their education.

Even in the early days of the university, students could study a broad scope of topics ranging from law to theology, engineering, arts and science, physical education, technical and vocational courses, music, medicine, pharmacy, dentistry, and more. Conwell felt that the greatest remedy for all the ills of both the poor and the rich was found in a proper education. In the early years, Temple also offered opportunities for students to take classes in order to earn their high school diplomas. Conwell felt that the countless masses who had made the mistake of not finishing school or who had had to discontinue their education for legitimate reasons should be given a second chance at an institution like Temple University.

He also felt that the church should play a substantial role in educating those whom the public does not educate. He believed that the church could help others by instituting evening classes during the week for the purpose of intellectual training that met the practical needs and desires of the people in the congregation, and it was, of course, in the church that the idea for Temple University was ultimately birthed when Charles M. Davies sought the advice of Conwell and the first class was begun.

A man of great faith, Conwell never let a lack of money or other obstacles stop him if he believed that God was leading him to do something. If a need was legitimate and justifiable, Conwell believed that the very need itself carried the inherent and potential power to supply the answer for the need.

When Conwell was in the beginning stages of building the great institution, there were many major challenges and obstacles that he had to overcome. He once explained to his biographer how many of these challenges stemmed from the insecurities of the wealthy elite:

> The enterprise has had its dark days, when great sacrifices were necessary for its continuance. It has had the opposition of some employers who feared that an education would turn their employees into other occupations, and it has had the prejudice of the rich who naturally desire to keep the higher places of earth for their sons and daughters, and who often stated that they feared the institution was educating the common people "above their station" and would lead the poor people to be ambitious for places which could only be occupied to advantage by the wealthy.
>
> While the rich institutions of the land received millions and millions from the gifts of the wealthy and seemed to have more money floating into their treasuries than they were able to administrate, yet the Temple University, without endowment and without gifts of the rich, kept steadily rising to favor and to power, until the natural rise in the value of property

given to it laid the foundation for a permanent institution and landed it safely beyond the danger of financial wreck.

Temple, one of Conwell's greatest contributions to the city of Philadelphia, was indeed one of a kind and the first of its kind. When it was started, the mere fact that students flooded the gates to enroll confirmed that it met a great need. There was no need to entice or manipulate anyone to attend for the purpose of increasing enrollment. Students simply came, and the institution grew and grew out of a natural need. In Conwell's lifetime alone, more than 100,000 students attended the university, a remarkable accomplishment in that day.

What made Temple remarkably unique was that it wasn't designed as a school for society's elite. Most of the school's graduates were common working men and women with dramatic success stories of how going to school part-time at Temple had revolutionized their career opportunities and dramatically increased their earning power.

One woman who made a very low weekly income once came to Conwell and asked him to show her how to make more money. Conwell was impressed with the young lady's ambition and forthrightness in asking him for advice, but there was one thing that he noticed while he was talking to her that made him a bit skeptical: She was wearing a very expensive-looking hat. Was she a woman who was not able to improve her conditions because she was a poor steward of her financial resources?

Conwell was not opposed to people bettering their lives in order to have the better things of life, and he also viewed the Bible as a book that was in favor of advancement and success. He was just wondering if the lady with the very expensive hat had her priorities in order.

Since he was not a man who was quick to pass judgment without knowing the whole story, he took the time to get a full understanding of the woman's situation. Upon inquiring in a tactful manner, Conwell was surprised to discover that the young lady had made the beautiful hat herself. In an instant, his reservations were done away with and he immediately knew how to advise her to improve her financial circumstances. If she could make a beautiful hat like that for herself, she could easily do the same for others. Her key to success sat right on her own head in the form of a hat, and Conwell advised her to "go into millinery as a business."

A millinery course that was designed to train individuals in the making or selling of women's hats was already offered at Temple University, and Conwell recommended it to her. The young woman was ecstatic because she had never known that such a course was available. It was a discovery that would open new doors of opportunity for her, and she was even more elated to find out that she could take the course while she continued to work at her present job.

THE RUSSELL CONWELL STORY

After the woman graduated from Temple, she relocated and opened her own millinery business and became very successful. She wrote Conwell a letter informing him that her profit for one particular year was twenty-three times more than what she had made on a weekly basis at the job she had before going to school at Temple. In other words, it would be the equivalent of a person in our day getting a raise from $100 a week to $2,300 a week!

In another instance, while Conwell was the university president, one particular young man from another city heard about Temple and came to Philadelphia with only thirty cents in his pocket with hopes of attending the university. This young man, who had come to the school in poverty, eventually graduated from Temple and became a judge.

Throughout Conwell's administration, there were also countless other inspiring testimonies of teachers who studied at Temple and later became professors, office boys who became bank presidents, and a street cleaner who became a mayor. One could conclude that Conwell's greatest success was giving of himself to inspire a multitude of others to succeed.

The institution was chartered in 1888 with 590 students, and at that time classes were held in the basement of the church and in two adjacent houses. When the college had to turn students away for lack of space, Conwell called on his congregation to help take the institution to the next level. Just as his faithful and devoted congregation had helped him to build the church from virtually nothing, they gave sacrificially to an investment fund to further the progress of the college. Children brought their spare change, women sold their jewelry, and families cut down on their grocery expenses in order to have more to give. Other contributions included $400 from factory workers who gave fifty cents each and $2,000 from police officers who gave a dollar each. Eventually the state of Pennsylvania contributed a sizable sum of money on an annual basis, but in the early years not many large contributions were received. Temple was indeed a university for the people, built by the people. In 1893, thanks to the sacrificial giving from the people, the building project for the college came into fruition.

When the cornerstone of the college building was laid in August of 1893, Conwell made this declaration:

> Friends, today we do something more than simply lay the corner-stone of a college building. We do an act here very simply that shows to the world—and will go on testifying after we have gone to our long rest—that the Church of Jesus Christ is not only an institution of theory but an institution of practice. It will stand here upon this great broad street and say through the coming years to all passersby, "Christianity means something for the good of humanity; Christianity means not only belief in things that are good and pure and righteous, but it also means an activity that shall bless those

who need the assistance of others." It shall say to the rich man, "Give thou of thy surplus to those who have not." It shall say to the poor man, "Make thou the most of thy opportunities and thou shalt be the equal of the rich."

Now, in the name of the people who have given for this enterprise; in the name of many Christians who have prayed, and who are now sending up their prayers to heaven, I lay this corner-stone.

In May 1894, the dedication services of Temple College (its name was not changed to Temple University until December 12, 1907, due to an amendment in the charter) took place in celebration of its new home, which would provide much more space for the throngs of students who were eager to attend.

Initially, classes were offered for free, but eventually a small fee had to be charged to ward off the element of shiftless individuals who were not serious about getting an education. Also, Conwell believed that a great sense of accomplishment resulted when a person was able to earn his education by paying his own way through school.

The university was attended by virtually every nationality representing almost every occupation. Conwell did not like some of the red tape he had to deal with during his days as a student at Yale, so it was his objective to offer Temple students educational courses that were convenient to their schedules and budgets. The administration shared Conwell's philosophy of changing plans or adapting to the needs of the students in order to serve as many people as possible.

Over the years, the university continued to grow as new facilities were added to meet an increased demand. When it was founded, Temple was primarily designed as a college for "those who must earn as they learn." More than a century after its inception, Temple University is still attended by many working individuals who take classes part-time, but it also obviously attracts thousands of full-time students from all classes of people.

Biographer Robert Shackleton pointed out that Conwell was always big on giving credit to others and deflecting praise away from himself. His unselfish willingness to meet the needs of others is the primary reason that Temple University stands today, but it was typical of Conwell to give credit where credit was due—first to the Lord, then to all the volunteer instructors who were there in the very beginning: professors from the University of Pennsylvania, teachers from the public school system, and other devoted men and women. To Conwell, instruction and inspiration were great needs of humanity, and Temple University helped him to meet those needs in an affordable fashion.

8
THE HOSPITALS
RUSSELL CONWELL
STARTED AND MANAGED

While Conwell was pastoring, building a new church, and establishing a university all at the same time, he felt another great need, which compelled him to take on even greater challenges. He constantly saw so many sick people in his congregation and in the neighborhood who were poor and unable to afford proper medical care that he was moved with compassion to help them. Since there was not a large hospital with up-to-date equipment in the vicinity, Conwell was motivated to help because he felt that it was within his purpose and power to do so.

In virtually every endeavor he started, Conwell's beginning was very small. As one of his biographers once pointed out, most men would probably never start anything because of a need to wait until a big beginning could be made. Conwell dreamed of big things in his future, but he was always ready to begin immediately on a very small scale, no matter what others may have thought.

Just as it was with the founding of Temple University, with no big plans or grandiose ideas, the Samaritan Hospital was started when Conwell and his associates simply reached out to help one person. Explaining to biographer Agnes Rush Burr how the hospital was formed, Conwell said:

> The Samaritan Hospital, which has become one of the great agencies for the healing of the sick poor in the city of Philadelphia, has been one of those mysterious developments which it is impossible to account for in the usual conditions of life. A young woman was seriously ill, with a very dangerous and somewhat infectious disease of the mouth. Her case was a very disagreeable and difficult one to care for in the home where she had lived as an orphan. The physician in charge suggested to me that the only reasonable way to care for the poor, afflicted woman was to hire two rooms in the upper story of some private house and put her in charge of a trained nurse.
>
> We rented two such rooms and that one patient and those two rooms were the beginning of the Samaritan Hospital which now reaches so many thousands of the poor in the course of a year, because we soon hired the whole house. Then we purchased it with a small payment down, furnished

it with gifts from our congregation, and found young women who desired training in the actual practice of nursing. Soon we were overwhelmed with physicians who offered their services free in such work.

We were soon so crowded that we were encouraged to purchase the adjoining dwelling, which was on the corner of Broad and Ontario Streets, Philadelphia. That we also purchased with a small payment and held for some time on a large mortgage. Afterwards we purchased a large lot north on Broad Street and then a similar lot on Park Avenue, after which the State of Pennsylvania came forward with appropriations for the maintenance of the hospital in its efforts to care for the poor people of the state.

Then one building after another arose as if by magic. Money came in from unexpected quarters, which, with some special subscriptions on the part of those most interested in the hospital, made the institution a permanent part of the humanitarian work of Philadelphia. Like all the other institutions, missions and enterprises which our church undertook to found or support, it started—as in the creation—with nothing; was "without form and void," and grew into something by a mysterious but powerful Providence which seemed to push us on with the work beyond our plans or highest hopes. Where the spirit of life is, something must grow.

He also explained to Burr the purpose of the hospital and its work:

The hospital was founded, and this property purchased, in the hope that it would do Christ's work. Not simply to heal for the sake of professional experience; not simply to cure disease and repair broken bones; but to so do those charitable acts as to enforce the truth Jesus taught, that God "would not that any should perish, but that all should come unto Him and live." Soul and body, both need the healing balm of Christianity. The hospital modestly and touchingly furnishes it to all classes, creeds and ages whose sufferings cause them to cry out, "Have mercy on me."

The hospital opened on February 1, 1892, and it was the intent of its founders to never turn anyone away for lack of money if at all possible. Services were given free of charge to individuals of all races and creeds who had no money, but Conwell did not believe in giving handouts to those who could afford to pay something. He felt that this was not fair to his medical staff and also felt that it would encourage wrong attitudes in the patients. Consequently, the hospital adopted a policy that those who could afford it would pay according to their income. Conwell wanted the patients to come to the understanding that charity was only meant to be a temporary form of assistance rather than a permanent support, unless the person in need was truly helpless.

He was opposed to the type of charitable organizations that enabled the lazy swindlers or cons to remain in the dependent state of mind, and he felt that it was wrong to give to "itinerant beggars" who thought that the world owed them something. Many of the public charitable institutions of his time, from his view, were "not charities at all." They merely crippled people for life with a beggar's mentality. In gathering research on these matters, Conwell discovered that the majority of individuals who applied for assistance at various institutions were "impostors ... and many are swindlers and professional burglars." To avoid catering to the swindler as much as possible, the rules were strictly enforced at the Samaritan Hospital. However, the hospital staff was sensitive and skilled at taking a personal interest in each person and treating patients with a type of dignity that would cause the sick to feel like something more than just a number.

At the time, most hospitals only had weekday visiting hours, but Conwell personally ordered more flexible weekend and night visiting hours to accommodate the normal working people and the poor. It was in his nature to always make the necessary adjustments to better meet the needs of the others if it was in his power to do so.

The Samaritan Hospital was also on the cutting edge for its day and time. Top physicians and well-known specialists gave of their services, utilizing modern equipment, and there was a large number of beds and rooms for the sick. Those who freely gave of themselves to make the Samaritan Hospital possible were indeed "good Samaritans"—just like the man in the Bible who went out of his way to help a sick and suffering stranger.

In addition to founding the Samaritan Hospital, Conwell also helped to expand and manage the Garretson and Greatheart hospitals in Philadelphia. His ability to stay on top of a multitude of major responsibilities and remain the active leader of several organizations with the limited amount of hours in a day was viewed by some as miraculous.

9

HOW RUSSELL CONWELL'S MOST POPULAR MESSAGE INFLUENCED MILLIONS

Despite all of his great accomplishments, Russell Conwell is probably recognized best for his famous "Acres of Diamonds" message (reprinted in part 2 of this book). He admitted that it was his most spontaneous lecture and that he spent the least amount of time to prepare it, but that it had the greatest success with his audiences worldwide. He also pointed out that some of the lectures that he spent months researching and preparing were the ones that achieved the least success.

Conwell himself could have never anticipated the enormous impact the "Acres of Diamonds" message would have on the world during his day and even after his death. During his lifetime, he felt that it was his duty to help as many individuals as possible to discover purpose. It was his belief that each person has a unique purpose and that it is every individual's personal responsibility to find and fulfill that purpose by discovering the "acres of diamonds" right in his or her own backyard.

At the core of the "Acres of Diamonds" message was the theme that countless people often overlook the valuable treasures right in their midst because they are too busy looking far off for a get-rich-quick scheme. When communicating to audiences, Conwell explained that the "acres of diamonds" right in one's own backyard could very well be a simple talent that a person possessed, an ability to invent something, or the ability to supply a basic need that could cause one to profit or achieve wealth.

It was not likely that Conwell ever shared the "Acres of Diamonds" message without telling the very captivating and amusing tale of an ancient Persian farmer by the name of Ali Hafed who sold his farm and exhausted all of his resources traveling the world in a search for diamonds. His treasure hunt was unsuccessful, and the impoverished and frustrated Ali Hafed committed suicide and never returned to his homeland. After Ali Hafed had taken his own life, however, the man who had purchased his property discovered that there were acres of diamonds right in Ali Hafed's own backyard! As one Pennsylvania newspaper of Conwell's day stated, "In substance, the theme of 'Acres of Diamonds' is that people listening to idle tales of 'easy money' to be had somewhere far away are apt to neglect the wealth that lies all around them awaiting development."

Millions Inspired to Fill Needs

When delivering his "Acres of Diamonds" message, Conwell would share a number of astonishing true stories of individuals who had sold property and moved to faraway places to seek riches, only to later discover that the property they had sold was filled with millions of dollars worth of gold, oil, or silver. As a result of this message, a myriad of individuals were inspired to search for the "acres of diamonds" right in their own backyards, and many stunning transformations took place. Entire towns and regions were revitalized; factories were started; villages turned into cities; banks were established; schools and colleges were opened; churches were founded and built; countless young men and women furthered their educations; depressed and discouraged individuals who had failed started over and became successful; men behind prison walls read copies of the lecture and used it to change their lives for the better; books were written and new authors were discovered; men and women drifting through life received greater purpose and direction; teachers were made; and speakers took to the platform to effect positive change.

Some of the more specific transformations that took place during Conwell's era included the following: A baker got wealthy by taking the initiative to conceive a plan for an improved oven. A teacher was inspired to more effectively teach what his students needed to know by adding agricultural chemistry to the curriculum, and the teacher moved up the ranks to principal, superintendent, and eventually university president. A young pastor from Texas who was thirty-six years old and had a congregation of 500 members was inspired by Conwell's message years before he started the church. A former inmate who was not sure if he could overcome his past heard the lecture and wrote to Conwell for advice, and after taking heed to Conwell's council, he became a respectable member of the community and was a member of Congress for sixteen years. A discouraged woman on an unprofitable farm grabbed hold of the message, became an authority on stock raising, and made millions of dollars in net profits. A man sold his very first order of 1,600 puddings to a large wholesale grocery firm after hearing the message and receiving advice from Conwell to consider his wife's delicious plum pudding as his "acres of diamonds." Poor farmers were transformed into wealthy men by following Conwell's advice to "raise what the people around you need."

On one occasion when Conwell was giving his famous lecture, a bank teller from North Carolina perked up when he heard Conwell say, "Your wealth is too near you; you are right over it." Right there on the spot the bank teller noticed that the lady directly in front of him had on a large hat and immediately felt that his wealth might be in that hat. As the man continued to listen to the lecture, Conwell commented, "Wherever there is a human need there is a great fortune." At that moment, the bank teller suddenly got an idea for a better hatpin than the one the woman was wearing. The pin was eventually manufactured and the man was awarded $55,000 for a patent on a simple hatpin.

On another occasion, a lady who had bought a small, cheap farm with her husband heard Conwell's lecture and laughingly said to herself, "There are no acres of diamonds on this place!" One day, however, she spotted a spring of really good quality water on the property. She and her husband had not really noticed it when they first bought the land. Because Conwell's lecture had inspired her to keep her eyes open for the acres of diamonds in her own backyard, she had the water analyzed and discovered that it was of a very pure quality. Before she knew it, the woman was getting the water bottled and making good money selling it as a special brand of spring water.

Conwell also shared the account of a time when he gave the "Acres of Diamonds" message at a church that was struggling with overwhelming debt and about to go under. While he was giving the part of the message about how people could take action to help an entire town, he appealed to the congregation. He simply stated that if fifty people would fully pledge a certain amount of money, the church could pay off its debt and grow to be a transforming force in the community. Forty-one of the people at the service committed to the pledge, and the church eventually paid all its debts, grew larger, and became one of the most successful forces in the town.

The following is an actual letter that was written to Conwell by a man in Detroit who greatly benefited from the "Acres of Diamond" message:

> On your last trip to Detroit I was present at your lecture, "Acres of Diamonds," and, needless to say, I was greatly inspired by it, as were also some brother salesmen who accompanied me. When my wife and I went home that evening we discussed the possibility of finding some "sure enough" diamonds here in Detroit. I am a salesman for a well-known device for writing checks—such as your banks in Philadelphia use. Well, a few days after your lecture here, I was calling on a prospect in one of the office buildings, when it was suggested that I interview a certain professional man in that building. I called on this man and sold him one of our devices, whereupon he asked me why I didn't call on all the other men in town in the same line. I took a list of a few of these men and sold to most of them.
>
> Then I began an investigation, the result of which is that there are something like 175,000 uncalled-on prospects—all high-grade men, and men who are making big incomes—just the very kind who need a device for the protection of their checks. I at once began to specialize on this class of prospects to the exclusion of all other work. This I did for over three months, meeting with such fine success that our company recently has sent

me out to the various large city offices to instruct our salesmen in selling to this new line of prospective customers.

A few weeks ago I visited your own city, where I found over five thousand professional men of the class mentioned, none of whom had ever been sold to, and I instructed the local men there how to approach and sell these men. We expect that two men will be kept busy on this line of work alone for many months right in Philadelphia, and that other salesmen all over the United States will be likewise engaged for the remainder of 1916; furthermore, we anticipate that the men engaged in this special work will earn in commissions $100,000.

And your auditor of last fall is now going around the country translating your lecture into the terms of our business and showing our salesmen that truly there are "Acres of Diamonds" in their own localities. I may say that, in giving my little talk to our selling organization, I mentioned that my own researches were inspired by your great lecture. As a matter of fact, I have taken the liberty of quoting from your wonderful lecture in my own little talk, which I call "Nuggets of Gold." Thus does your work go on. Of course, in all these years your mail has been filled with such letters of appreciation as this from all over the country, but I know that you will be glad to have this one additional message of thanks from me.

This letter tells of just one incident out of countless thousands that took place as a result of the "Acres of Diamonds" message during Conwell's lifetime alone. The positive results achieved through his message—which was delivered throughout the United States and all over the world—even during his lifetime are incalculable, and we have not even begun to discuss the many thousands or even millions more who have been transformed by reading the lecture in the many years following Conwell's passing. Conwell traveled around the globe proclaiming the message that anyone can be successful by simply "supplying a need," and his enormous success with the message came because the lecture itself supplied the need in every man and woman to discover purpose by finding the "acres of diamonds" right in their own backyards.

During his lifetime, Conwell dedicated a great part of his existence to making a difference in the lives of a multitude of people who went through life lacking direction, purpose, or hope. Even now, a whole new generation of individuals can be inspired to take hold of the timeless "Acres of Diamonds" message in order to turn dreams into reality and soar to new heights.

Why the "Penniless Millionaire" Gave It All Away

While so many other successful individuals focused on their own personal accumulation of wealth, Conwell's chief ambition in life was not to accumulate a huge amount of material possessions or to amass a large personal bank account for himself. On the contrary, his greatest ambition was to spread the "Acres of

Diamonds" vision in order that countless others could prosper and also learn that the highest form of prosperity was in helping others.

Conwell, known by many as the "penniless millionaire," did not personally receive any large fees for his work, nor did he have a bank account that he could point to as a sign of his success. Recognized as a builder of men through his lectures and his charitable giving, Conwell never kept one dollar of the enormous amount of profits he made over the years from giving the lecture. It was calculated that during his career, he earned a total of about $8 million from his "Acres of Diamonds" lecture, all of which he donated for the education of poor students. In the context of our times, some would estimate $8 million to be the equivalent of about $300 million today!

In addition to the financial sacrifices he made, Conwell often sacrificed his own physical comfort for the benefit of others. Many are not aware that he experienced some extreme discomforts during more than sixty years of travel on the lecture circuit. Year in and year out during his extensive travels, without profiting from any of the proceeds for his lectures, he endured exhausting delays, extreme cold, blizzards, blazing heat, sub-par railroads, inferior food, poor travel conditions, little or no sleep while rushing from one engagement to the next, and hours without access to food. Once, he even fell and broke his arm while rushing to a lecture. Not allowing the injury to deter him, he simply wrapped up the injured arm and gave his speech. On another occasion, when Conwell was more than seventy years old, he stayed in a hotel with no heat in ten-below-zero weather in order to give a lecture so that he would not let down a student who really needed the money. There were very few professional speakers during Conwell's day (and even in today's time) who would have been willing to endure such hardships even for top dollar. But Russell Conwell endured so that he could give his money away for the benefit of others.

Conwell one day explained to biographer Agnes Rush Burr how he made the decision to donate his lecture proceeds to poor students:

> I had been visiting the scenes of my own college days at Yale. As I stood in the room where I had lived in such poverty, as I went through the dining-room and kitchen of the house where, in the old days, I had to be on duty at four-thirty in the morning to help make everything ready; as I went through the college halls and classrooms where I had shunned my classmates because of my shabby, ragged clothes, I thought of those hard, bitter days of work and poverty; of the long, exhausting hours I was compelled to spend in working and struggling; of my humiliation and keen suffering of mind and spirit at my appearance and need, compared with the rich boys about me.
>
> I traveled on to Boston, but the picture of those days and all I had suffered stayed with me. I went to Tremont Temple Church. No one was in it. In the twilight gloom of that great church and the stillness that reigned

there, I knelt and vowed to give thenceforth the proceeds from my lectures to poor students, so that at least some of those struggling for an education might never know the suffering and humiliation I had endured.

The "penniless millionaire" never really thought about how much he had actually given away over the years until a colleague decided to calculate the numbers. Conwell's greatest profits and rewards were the countless people whose lives were revolutionized as a result of the "Acres of Diamonds" message. He was perhaps the richest man in the world without a bank account from which to draw. Conwell would simply forward the lecture proceeds to the student to whom it was promised, and that was that. All in all, he helped about 10,000 young men in their educational pursuits.

When Conwell mailed a check from his "Acres of Diamonds" proceeds in order to help a student, he always sent a letter giving the student some practical advice and also telling the student "that he is to feel under no obligation except to his Lord." He never attempted to send any students enough for all their expenses, but his intent was to help them avoid the type of hardship that he had to endure. This was another aspect of Conwell's life work in which he wanted to keep things simple, so he did not seek to complicate matters by requiring any type of reports or returns on his investment. He simply wanted to help people for the sake of helping them, and he did not want to hold over their heads a sense of obligation to him personally.

Overwhelming Gratitude

It was not uncommon for Conwell to meet various individuals who would thank him for helping them to get an education. At one lecture event, a man who was assigned to introduce Conwell had to leave the platform before he could finish his introduction because he was overwhelmed and moved to tears as he told about the check he had received that helped him to finish school during very hard times. Another young man who had become the principal of a high school introduced himself as one of Conwell's "boys" because he had gotten the opportunity to receive an education after receiving a check from Conwell.

One Philadelphia newspaper writer of Conwell's era wrote:

> No man can reckon the indebtedness of Philadelphia to this admirable citizen who might have been a plutocrat, but chose instead, for the sake of others, to reserve only a modest competency for himself out of all the vast accumulation. His satisfaction as he looks back over the course of his life must be keen, when he thinks of the gratitude he has earned, where others were content to earn and hoard mere dollars. This man's golden treasury is reckoned in the bright mintage of ever-living gratitude for lives enabled to reach their fullest development of usefulness.

THE RUSSELL CONWELL STORY

Conwell also told of a strange yet amusing experience of a young man he met one night at a train station in the state of Washington. The man had been to a couple of "Acres of Diamonds" lectures and was so inspired that he told Conwell that he was able to perform the lecture word for word. Sure enough, using the same hand gestures, the same exact words, and the very tone of voice of Conwell himself, the man began to perform right in front of Conwell in the dark of the night. Conwell recalled that it was one of the eeriest feelings he had ever had, but he was extremely amused. It was almost as if he had an out-of-body experience and was watching himself speak until the train came and the man stopped. He once laughingly remarked that if he ever needed an understudy to take his place, he knew where to find this man.

It also amused Conwell when some people would mistakenly refer to his famous "Acres of Diamonds" lecture as "Ace of Diamonds." But the fact that the "Acres of Diamonds" message influenced millions during Conwell's lifetime and is still influencing millions today is certainly not to be mistaken.

In 1913, on Conwell's seventieth birthday, he gave the "Acres of Diamonds" lecture for the five-thousandth time at the Academy of Music in Philadelphia to a jam-packed audience of thousands. He had come a long way since he fist delivered the lecture to a few hundred people back in the 1800s. Before Conwell passed away, he had delivered the lecture more than 6,000 times to live audiences and on the radio.

10

HOW RUSSELL CONWELL BECAME THE GREATEST MOTIVATIONAL SPEAKER OF HIS TIME

Although Conwell was basically described as a lecturer in his day, if he were around today he would more than likely be identified by some as a motivational speaker due to the nature of the "Acres of Diamonds" message. And, in light of his accomplishments—even without the avenues of mass media that we have available today—he can be considered the greatest motivational speaker of his time. A pamphlet printed during the height of Russell Conwell's illustrious career stated: "More special trains are run to Conwell's lectures every year than to any other single attraction in the United States. Within nineteen years over five thousand people have joined his church in Philadelphia."

When Conwell was just a small child he demonstrated his fascination with public speaking by practicing his speeches on cats, dogs, roosters, cows, horses, and other farm animals. He recalled that he practiced his speeches so much as a kid that his sister and his neighbors were sometimes annoyed at hearing him. Just for the sake of getting experience, he eventually began speaking to just about any type of human audience that would receive him, and when he lectured at graduation ceremonies, country fairs, and other events, he was sometimes compensated with such items as a ham or a jack-knife.

It is estimated that over the course of his entire professional lecturing career Conwell spoke to 10 million people and was the most popular speaker in the world during his time based on the statistics of the lecture bureaus. He also gave many other lectures in addition to his most popular "Acres of Diamonds" message, and he was offered large sums of money to lecture in places all over the world, including China, Japan, Italy, India, Israel, England, Germany, Switzerland, France, Turkey, and Egypt. In the United States he spoke to all races and classes of people, and he also spoke to blacks at institutes in the South.

The newspaper writers who witnessed one of Conwell's lectures described him as a speaker who was so powerfully eloquent and so mesmerizing that he made audiences unconscious of time. Those who reported his lectures sometimes described his facial expressions as more descriptive and telling than the very words he spoke. He was also described by writers of his day as a man who sometimes left his audiences roaring with convulsions of laughter. One particular newspaper writer who attended a lecture also pointed out that Conwell captivated his audiences with tales of his encounters with famous men, while nothing compared to the passion and purity his face displayed when he referred to his Maker. He was also described by some to be the only lecturer in America who could come to certain cities and fill an auditorium with thousands of people paying to hear him speak.

A Massachusetts newspaper declared, "It is useless to try to report Dr. Conwell's lectures. They are unique. Unlike anything or any one else. Filled with good sense; brilliant with new suggestions; and inspiring always to noble life and deeds. They always please with their wit. The reader of his addresses does not know the full power of the man."

Although Conwell preached a practical gospel of wealth and prosperity at times, he was not a preacher of prosperity whose messages focused on personal material possessions like big houses, fancy automobiles, and personal assets. He never alienated his listeners by flaunting his personal belongings or accomplishments but always focused his efforts on what could be done to help others.

In addition, Conwell avoided spending his time criticizing those who decided to live in great luxury. In his "Acres of Diamonds" message, he even pointed out that some of the "very best people in character as well as in enterprise" were individuals with "beautiful homes with gardens and flowers, those magnificent homes so lovely in their art." But his main focus was always on the concept of utilizing one's resources for the purpose of serving humanity.

Although he did not use notes and did not even think about his lectures very much during the day, Conwell certainly was not a man who did not believe in preparation. His preparation simply took place during all the years he spent researching, studying, and reading about his topics. He was gifted in the extemporaneous style of speaking, and when it was time for him to give a lecture, the information that came out of his mouth was the result of years of reading and research related to his topic. It was only on rare occasions, especially if a lecture was new or if he had not given it in years, that Conwell would use a few notes or a basic outline.

Conwell never lacked information due to inadequate preparation. On the contrary, his greater challenge was sometimes having so much information that he was not sure how to share it in one lecture alone. Due to the abundance of information and illustrations, he would sometimes give "Acres of Diamonds" over the course of three lectures. He had so many relevant illustrations to share that he hardly ever gave a lecture the same way twice. Even if a listener had heard Conwell speak on the same topic more than once, Conwell would always come forth with fresh new illustrations fit for the occasion.

THE RUSSELL CONWELL STORY

Conwell advised those interested in being effective orators to simply be natural. From all of his experiences and studies of the art of public speaking, he considered being natural one of the most important things a speaker can do to be successful. He also encouraged public speakers to do what worked best for them in terms of being extemporaneous or following a manuscript.

Conwell utilized quite a few illustrations and parables in his messages because he always felt that people were more impressed by illustrations than by arguments, and most of the illustrations he used were based on his own unique experiences or encounters. In one instance, he referred to something he heard a child say earlier in the week; the next minute he mentioned that Elias Howe personally told Conwell that it was Howe's wife who had invented the sewing, machine although most people gave Howe the credit. Conwell's credible, relevant, and simple illustrations added a personal element to his messages that captivated his audiences all the more. He once said to his congregation, "I want to preach so simply that you will not think it preaching, but just that you are listening to a friend."

He never hesitated to use humor in his messages but cautioned orators against the type of laughter that got the audience off track or distracted them from the significance of a message. In a little book Conwell published for students regarding the study of oratory, he stated, "It is easy to raise a laugh, but dangerous, for it is the greatest test of an orator's control of his audience to be able to land them again on the solid earth of sober thinking."

Conwell was also perceptive enough to understand that any public speaker who did not charge a certain type of fee for his services could easily open himself up for exploitation. He was aware of the reality that many people fail to properly appreciate or respect a service if they do not pay for it and even perceive a service to be worth a lot more if they pay more for it. He said, "I found that if I would retain my influence with those I wished to benefit, I must continually insist upon an adequate return for the labor expended, although the fees did not go into my personal account." Conwell related this principle to the story Henry Ward Beecher told of the time he spoke for $5,000 to raise funds for some female employees in St. Louis who had been injured on the job. Beecher explained to Conwell that the way the event turned out demonstrated how much more the people understood and appreciated his speech because they had to raise $5,000 before he would take the platform.

Conwell further expressed his views to biographer Agnes Rush Burr regarding this issue:

> Public speakers and ministers of the Gospel often defeat their own righteous ambitions by cheapening themselves under such circumstances and refusing to receive money, showing by their own estimate the value of their work, and destroying the influence of their own teaching. An overestimate of one's value, which is perhaps the most dangerous thing, is, of

course, a very foolish condition of mind and leads to sure defeat. The most of the sins of our world are sins of the extremists.

Although Conwell had gained the admiration of millions as a lecturer, there still seemed to be that certain class of haughty people who did not care for him. Conwell had great relationships with some of the richest men in the country, and he was also greatly admired by millions of the common people, but there seemed to be a class in between that failed to recognize Conwell, perhaps because they did not care to relate to a man who was so concerned about ordinary people. Conwell's greatest hope was simply that no one would enter into his life without being benefited.

When Conwell was in his seventies, at the height of his popularity, he still occasionally took speaking engagements for small fees in towns that were not likely to be visited by a high-profile speaker like himself. He felt that some of the smaller areas of the country had the greatest need for motivation and change, so he made the sacrifice of dealing with the discomforts and substandard conditions that came with traveling to them. He could have easily chosen to take only the big engagements, but Conwell was always thinking about those who were less privileged. He was always on the move primarily for the purpose of helping others.

Even during his time of summer "vacation," it was not uncommon for him to lecture every day and preach on Sundays for several consecutive months without any breaks. And when he traveled, he was continually brightening someone's day with his kind words or actions. The hotel clerk, the waitress in the restaurant, or the conductor on the train were just some of the countless strangers he inspired in passing. It was easily apparent that everywhere he went he loved people, and people always responded to his love.

To Conwell, public speaking was the most enjoyable profession to be had. He sometimes talked about the indescribable heights of experience that came when a speaker totally lost himself in the process of communicating life-changing concepts to a receptive audience. Toward the end of his life, Conwell expressed the view that he could have accomplished more during his younger years if he had made lecturing his only profession and abandoned all other business endeavors.

Although he admitted that it was perhaps a personal eccentricity, Conwell was grateful that he did not have to earn his living through the sacred acts of lecturing and preaching. He once said to Burr, "I do not mean to say it is dishonorable or a matter for criticism, when men are obliged to earn their living by public speech. But it has been a blessing beyond all compare to feel that I can go up on the platform and say to the people what I felt it was most necessary to say, and to say it in my own way, free from all connection with wages, or money reward."

11
THE GREATEST SERMON RUSSELL CONWELL EVER PREACHED

Russell Conwell was definitely not a perfect man. This does not mean that we know of some great scandal in his life, but only that it is a simple truth that there is no human who ever existed on this earth who was perfect. The very Bible that Conwell so deeply believed in declares, "All have sinned, and come short of the glory of God" (Romans 3:23). It is a mere reality to conclude that, throughout his lifetime, Conwell doubtless said and did some things—whether big or small—that he later regretted.

Thus, it is not the intent of this book to paint a picture of Conwell as a perfect saint. However, in studying his life and work, it is evident that Conwell was a genuine, practical, and balanced Christian leader who made a major impact in the world.

Biographer Robert Shackleton pointed out that he never heard a friend criticize Conwell for anything but for giving too much of himself. Shackleton also said that though Conwell was extremely eloquent when necessary, his actions always seemed to speak louder than his words. For example, even though he had a great love for his country, Conwell was never boastful about America. Rarely did he speak about patriotism or being a good citizen, but he quietly kept an American flag hanging in the church and in his home.

Though Conwell was not without his critics, there were many credible and noble men during his time who spoke very highly of him. Charles A. Dana, a contemporary of Conwell's who was a famous *New York Sun* editor, once wrote a letter of recommendation to Harper & Brothers Publishers in praise of Conwell's ability as a writer and his high degree of modesty. The letter stated:

> As a writer of biographies, Doctor Conwell has no superior. Indeed, I can say considerately, that he is one of America's greatest men. He never advertises himself; never saves a newspaper clipping concerning himself; never keeps a sermon of his own; and will not seek applause. You must go after him if you want him. He will not apply to you. He has written many books and has addressed more people than any other living man. To do this without writing or dictating a line to advertise himself is nothing else than the victory of a great genius. He is a gem worth your seeking, valuable

anywhere. I say again that I regard Russell H. Conwell, of Philadelphia, as America's greatest man in the best form. I cannot do your work; he can.

Another one of Conwell's contemporaries, legendary millionaire merchant John Wanamaker, had the following to say in an address he once gave:

> Doctor Conwell is a great citizen who cannot be matched in this or any other state. How proud and thankful is Philadelphia to own him! He had the vision years ago, not of building buildings, but of building men—citizenship.

A newspaper writer who was also a contemporary of Conwell's once stated, "He himself is more inspiring than anything he has ever said or done, despite all he has said and all he has done." And, according to biographer Agnes Rush Burr, a minister who was a friend to Conwell recalled that though there was much theological controversy and strife in the air during Conwell's later years, he never fed into it. In reference to Conwell's exemplary life, the minister remarked, "He did not attempt to define Christ, but to live like Him."

It seems that among the people who knew him best, the general consensus was that the way Conwell lived his life was the greatest sermon he ever preached.

In spite of the tremendous legacy he left behind, decades after his death there still seem to be those who would like to minimize Conwell's accomplishments. In his "Acres of Diamonds" lecture, Conwell boldly stated, "You ought to get rich, and it is your duty to get rich. Money is power, and you ought to be reasonably ambitious to have it. You ought because you can do more good with it than you could without it. Money will do good as well as harm." Due to the various Scriptures that admonish us to "seek ye first the kingdom of God, and his righteousness" (Matthew 6:33) and beware of the pain that can be caused by the deceitfulness of riches (see Mark 4:19; 1 Timothy 6:9-10), some perceived Conwell to be a greedy capitalist who was contradicting the very Bible he professed to believe.

Upon a full study of Conwell's life, however, it is very apparent that he understood that there is a danger in success if it is not kept in proper perspective. He also pointed out in his "Acres of Diamonds" message that money in and of itself is not evil, but that the love or worship of money is the root of all evil. "He who tries to attain unto it too quickly, or dishonestly, will fall into many snares, no doubt about that," said Conwell.

The Holy Bible that Conwell read taught him to guard against the corruptive influences that could come from getting riches the wrong way, but it also taught him that "thou shalt remember the LORD thy God: for it is he that giveth thee power to get wealth, that he may establish his covenant which he sware unto thy fathers, as it is this day" (Deuteronomy 8:18).

THE RUSSELL CONWELL STORY

In addition to the accusation that Conwell gave wealth improper priority, his very life was somewhat of a paradox, and this may have seemed confusing or contradictory, leading to criticism. On the one hand, Conwell was extremely wealthy. On the other hand, he was at times penniless during the height of his success and could not even draw from a bank account because he gave so much of his money away. It seems that Conwell fully understood that he was rich with a bank account in heaven because he had a direct connection with his Maker: "The earth is the LORD's, and the fulness thereof; the world, and they that dwell therein." (Psalm 24:1). He somehow knew that if he had a cause worth accomplishing, the Lord of the earth would make all of the resources at Conwell's disposal. And Conwell did not personally need a bank account on earth because of his tremendous ability to influence individuals to support his worthwhile causes. From the perspective of those who admired him, his life seemed to be a rare example of what true wealth or success is all about.

Conwell never implied, however, that a person who has no bank account is more spiritual or pious than one who does. In his famous lecture he even referred to a man who saves as one who "begins to leave off his bad habits and put money in the bank." Although his abundance of sacrificial giving meant that he had little at times, Conwell obviously understood that it is good stewardship to save money, and he was not the type who would try to force others to make the same personal sacrifices that he made. To Conwell, success at the highest level meant keeping priorities in order by seeking first the kingdom of God and using one's wealth to better serve humanity.

Other critics feel that Conwell at times was a shameless self-promoter because some of the stories he told about his own life seemed incredibly exaggerated or even unbelievable. Some scholars go so far as to say that there is no convincing evidence of Conwell's presence at Kenesaw Mountain, Georgia, during the Civil War. However, there is a legitimate and sensible explanation for this lack of proof, which Conwell gave to Burr: General McPherson unofficially appointed Conwell as lieutenant-colonel over Company D while Conwell was being court-martialed for unjust reasons. McPherson had intended to write to Lincoln to ask for a reversal of the court-martial decision, but McPherson was killed before the letter was written. The court-martial verdict was later reversed and Conwell received an honorable discharge. The untimely and sudden death of McPherson (who was killed in the battle of Atlanta on July 22, 1864), however, meant that Conwell was never officially recorded as having been a lieutenant-colonel with McPherson's army in the battle at Kenesaw Mountain.

Others have stated that there is no convincing evidence that Conwell's legendary orderly, John Ring, ever existed, as if to imply that Ring might have been a fictitious character contrived by Conwell for the sake of generating publicity.

However, there were many soldiers who actually fought with Conwell in the Civil War who could have come forward to expose such a lie if the story were indeed a falsehood. Furthermore, it was not only Conwell who told the story of John Ring, but his soldiers from Company D, who actually witnessed Ring's death and later reported the details.

In addition, it cannot be viewed as unusual that no official record of John Ring's birth exists, as in that particular time, record-keeping was not of the highest priority. There are plenty of famous persons whose births were not officially recorded but of whose existence we have ample evidence.

It is also interesting to point out that in Robert Shackleton's biographical account of Conwell's life, *His Life and Achievements*, published in 1915, there is an actual picture of Russell Conwell standing at the gravesite of the beloved John Ring. Shackleton also wrote that he once visited the grave of Ring in the town where Ring and Conwell both grew up:

> There is a little lonely cemetery in the Berkshires, a tiny burying-ground on a wind-swept hill, a few miles from Conwell's old home. In this isolated burying-ground bushes and vines and grass grow in profusion, and a few trees cast a gentle shade; and tree-clad hills go billowing off for miles and miles in wild and lonely beauty. And in that lonely little graveyard I found the plain stone that marks the resting-place of John Ring.

The implications that a man of Conwell's high moral character would need to hoodwink his audiences with false war stories or false testimonials about his conversion experience are unfortunate. Why was Conwell sharply criticized by so many individuals of his day, and why is he still criticized by some historians even today as an extremist, an exaggerator, or a man who was at times a reckless self-advertiser?

Perhaps one reason, as was mentioned in a previous chapter, is that many who criticized Conwell never actually met him or visited his church; they simply believed the criticisms that they heard from others.

Some would also argue that perhaps his critics are threatened by the legacy of his upstanding ethics, faith, and moral values and that Conwell's educational standards, which emphasize morality and biblical values as well as sound academic studies, pose a threat to some of the educators of our day to the point that they would prefer to leave him in the background.

Those who know Russell Conwell's history are constantly reminded of the reality of his faith by the great educational institution that he started from nothing, which is still thriving right in Philadelphia's own backyard. Conwell proved to be a minister of great integrity and a man of sound mind. Although he was devout in his commitment to the Lord, he always seemed to be more concerned about the impact of his actions rather than about his ability to speak with eloquence. Shackleton wrote:

THE RUSSELL CONWELL STORY

Deeply religious though he is, he does not force religion into conversation on ordinary subjects or upon people who may not be interested in it. With him, it is action and good works, with faith and belief, that count, except when talk is the natural, the fitting, the necessary thing; when addressing either one individual or thousands, he talks with superb effectiveness.

It is not difficult to see why some would misunderstand Conwell's radical statements and huge accomplishments to mean that he was sensational, boastful, extreme, or materialistic. Yet, with more than mere words alone, Conwell preached to the world by the way he lived. His very lifestyle taught millions that it is possible to possess great wealth without allowing the wealth to possess one's soul. It is important, then, to realize that it is impossible to fully understand or appreciate Conwell's viewpoints and deeds unless they are taken in the proper context of his life and times.

The very credible tributes from those who knew Conwell personally provide evidence that Conwell preached his greatest sermons not with words but by the way he lived his life. Every individual, no matter the race or creed, can receive outstanding benefits from learning the full story of the man who started Temple University from nothing and truly inspired millions of people to discover "acres of diamonds" in their own backyards.

12

FINAL INSIGHTS INTO THE LIFE OF A CHAMPION TO THE OPPRESSED

The sacrifices that Russell Conwell made brought many challenges in his personal and family life, but his persistent faith and patience allowed him to continually triumph in the midst of disappointments and setbacks. This final chapter will share some additional insights into the character and sacrificial lifestyle of the legendary "Acres of Diamonds" lecturer who fought a good fight until the very end.

Answered Prayer

Like all leaders, Conwell had his difficult moments and made mistakes that tempted him to give in to despair. But he always believed that God answers prayer. In the early days of his Philadelphia church, Conwell overrode the advice of some of his leaders and incurred a debt for an organ. Some of his colleagues had urged him to hold off from purchasing the organ until certain other expenses were met, but Conwell did not follow their advice because he was anxious to enhance the music program of the church.

After the church incurred the debt, a payment of $1,000 was desperately needed to prevent a lawsuit over an outstanding note. Conwell had signed the note personally, and if the money was not paid right away, it would cause him embarrassment and bring discouragement upon the church. Because he was young in the ministry and had not exercised the best judgment in purchasing the organ so soon, he could not appeal to his congregation for help. He attempted to get aid from friends, but he saw no sign of help anywhere. He did continue to pray, however, and the Lord granted him mercy. The very day that the holder of the note was going to begin proceedings against him, Conwell received a $1,000 donation from a man out west who knew nothing of his need. The man had simply found out through a relative about the great work Conwell's ministry was doing, and he wanted to offer general support.

At another time, when the Temple University buildings were in construction, $10,000 was desperately needed to pay a debt that was due within a few hours. The generous congregation was not rich and had already been stretched to the max in their giving, and it was uncommon for the very wealthy to aid Conwell in his ministry at that time. There was no one for Conwell to turn to, and despair was beginning to set in.

Because Conwell believed in success so much, it was difficult for him to deal with the possibility of failure. He preached success all throughout his life, and because he served a big God, he simply believed that it was just as easy to do big things as it was to do small things. He felt that a person should not be satisfied with small things in life, and one of his mottos was, "Think big things and then do them." But the "Acres of Diamonds" lecturer, who was accustomed to thinking big, left his administrative offices that day in a rare moment of despair.

When he got to his home a couple of blocks away, however, he found a check in the mail for exactly $10,000. Conwell ran back to his office, overflowing with exuberance and waving the check in his hand. It had come from a totally unexpected source. And, just as it had been with the man out west, the woman who sent the $10,000 check had no idea of the urgent need but simply wanted to support the ministry in a general way.

"Let Patience Have Her Perfect Work"

Conwell's favorite scriptural maxim was "Let patience have her perfect work." In fact, he repeated the maxim so much that he and his friends used to laugh about it. It constantly reminded him that he had to guard himself against impatience or anxiety while working to accomplish his goals. His ability to accomplish great things was his strength, but Conwell knew that it could also become a weakness that could lead him into anger and haste if he did not keep himself tempered and balanced.

Biographer Robert Shackleton pointed out that those who had long known Conwell said that they had never heard him censure anyone. Few of his colleagues had seen him angry or impatient, and he had a reputation of being a man who was self-controlled, with wonderful forbearance and kindness. He led so much by his powerful influence and example that people followed him with all willingness of heart. And Conwell was grateful and humbled when he thought of his accomplishments in spite of his shortcomings: "God and man have ever been very patient with me," he sometimes would say.

Alienation and Isolation

Once Conwell made up his mind to do something, he was not moved by the criticism of others. Whether or not that quality always worked to his advantage or was always appropriate for the situation can be debated, but his actions proved that he was certainly not a mere people-pleaser.

There was one particular incident that provides insight into Conwell's tenacity to stick to a decision once it was made, regardless of outside critics. The legendary "Acres of Diamonds" lecturer once received a very big diamond as a gift from an elderly deacon in his congregation whom he loved dearly. Conwell was not actually interested in wearing the diamond because he felt it was too big and obtrusive. He did wear it, however, because he did not want to hurt the deacon's feelings.

For years he was criticized sharply by some people for wearing the diamond, but he never tried to defend himself. When he finally stopped wearing the diamond, some people thought it was because the criticism had gotten to him. But Conwell admitted to Shackleton that he only stopped wearing the diamond because his beloved deacon had died.

In spite of his strength of character, Conwell was not a man who was immune to hurt and pain. He never let the unjust criticism of others stop him, but he sometimes alluded to the pain he felt. "When I have been hurt ... I have tried to let patience have her perfect work, for those very people, if you have patience with them, may afterward be of help."

During his early years in Philadelphia, he recalled how he felt the pain from ministers in his own denomination who misunderstood and misjudged him. Some of them accused Conwell of "making a circus of the church" because he was innovative, unique, and not bound to pointless traditions. But he was grateful that even some of his most bitter enemies had been won over with patience.

Shackleton referred to an encounter when a Philadelphia Baptist minister admitted with shame that all the ministers would ignore Conwell and refuse to greet him during ministers' meetings:

> "And it was all through our jealousy of his success," the minister said. "He came to this city a stranger, and he won instant popularity, and we couldn't stand it, and so we pounced upon things that he did that were altogether unimportant. The rest of us were so jealous of his winning throngs that we couldn't see the good in him. And it hurt Dr. Conwell so much that for ten years he did not come to our conferences. But all this was changed long ago. Now no minister is so welcomed as he is, and I don't believe that there ever has been a single time since he started coming again that he hasn't been asked to say something to us. We got over our jealously long ago and we all love him."

On another occasion, while speaking on his famous "Acres of Diamonds" topic, Conwell addressed the issue of why some people criticize others unjustly:

> Why is it Mr. Carnegie is criticized so sharply by an envious world? Because he has gotten more than we have. If a man knows more than I know, don't I incline to criticize somewhat his learning? Let a man stand in a pulpit and preach to thousands, and if I have fifteen people in my church, and they're all asleep, don't I criticize him? We always do that to the man who gets ahead of us.
>
> One of the richest men in this country came into my home and sat

down in my parlor and said: "Did you see all those lies about my family in the paper?"

"Certainly I did: I knew they were lies when I saw them."

"Why do they lie about me the way they do?"

"Well," I said to him, "if you will give me your check for one hundred millions, I will take all the lies along with it."

"Well," said he, "I don't see any sense in their thus talking about my family and myself. Conwell, tell me frankly, what do you think the American people think of me?"

"Well," said I, "they think you are the blackest-hearted villain that ever trod the soil!"

"But what can I do about it?"

There is nothing he can do about it and yet he is one of the sweetest Christian men I ever knew. If you get a hundred millions you will have the lies; you will be lied about, and you can judge your success in any line by the lies that are told about you.

Like all true leaders, Conwell had to deal with the painful sting of ruthless lies and criticism. Even more painful was the occasional alienation and isolation that he felt from many of his peers in ministry. But, he simply counted this as the price of being an innovative and progressive leader and did not let it stop him from doing the work he set out to do.

Championing Causes for the Underdogs

For Conwell, success meant serving others in spite of the criticism he sometimes received. He never forgot his struggles to get an education as a poor kid, and because he believed that certain unjust legislation made it difficult for poor individuals to get an education and enter the professional world, he spoke out on the issue just about everywhere he went. In one particular address he stated:

Bars are being raised to keep the poor boy out of the professions. If these obstacles are arbitrarily increased, we will eventually have in this country two classes—a peasant class and an aristocratic class. They may not be so named, but they will be so in fact. If I were starting today as I did fifty years ago—with nothing but health and determination to make my way into a profession—I could not succeed. I would reach a point where I could not pass without the open sesame of money.

Conwell believed that high standards in education were important, but he was concerned that the system was creating arbitrarily costly and stringent requirements that would prevent the underclass from qualifying for a higher education. Using the medical field as an example, he further stated his case:

I believe in proficiency. I believe fully in all the study and instruction and experimental and laboratory work possible. But I say, let examinations be the test of fitness—not hours in classrooms, or credentials from some "approved" college. Let the examinations be as rigid as possible. We cannot be too careful in licensing medical practitioners. But if a man can pass, give him his license, whether he has spent thirty-two hours in an actual classroom or has studied in the barn between chores, or in an attic half the night.

Suppose that, instead of keeping among my people and attending to the practical work of my church, I were compelled—in order to be allowed to preach—to study various doctrinal matters and examine the many theories of theology, what would become of the actual work that needs to be done? Let those fitted for higher research work and who want to do it, take it up. Let others who want to do a different kind of work have the opportunity to prepare for their work. We are in danger of getting into formalities—of insisting upon the letter and forgetting the spirit.

It will soon be that, unless a man or woman is a graduate of a school of journalism, he or she will find it difficult to obtain a position upon a newspaper; unless a man passes so many hours or weeks or years in a college classroom he will not be admitted to the bar. This is the lurking danger that I see—that not what a man knows will be the test; but whether he has spent so many hours a week—hours of daytime, too—in "approved" institutions, which must be richly endowed and consequently few in number. This means undoubtedly cutting the poor boy out.

Although Conwell's arguments might seem a bit radical for our time, in the context of his culture he was simply pointing out that what you know in a practical sense is more important than a piece of paper in the form of a college degree. Conwell was obviously all for higher education through colleges or universities because he himself had founded Temple University. He was merely concerned about seeing the concept of higher education taken to an extreme that would exclude the underprivileged from having equal opportunity and access to the type of education needed to gain lucrative employment. These were the types of issues that weighed on the heart of the man who spent so much of his lifetime championing causes for the underdogs.

Conwell also devoted some of his time to assisting blacks in their educational endeavors during a time when racism and discrimination were much more rampant in America. He lectured at black schools and colleges, and he was also instrumental in helping to start a school for young black women—the Spellman Academy (now Spellman College) in Atlanta, Georgia. In response to a plea from a friend in Atlanta, Conwell enlisted the help of educator Sophia B. Packard and secured the use of some government barracks, and the Spellman Academy was born, with Miss Packard as one of its cofounders.

In a nutshell, Conwell believed that in order for one to truly live, one must truly live for God. From his own personal experiences, he was acquainted with struggle, and he knew what it was to rely totally on the Master. With every venture he started, Conwell had lacked capital. Even when he decided to get his education at Yale, he launched out with virtually nothing but a dream. He had no capital when he came to Philadelphia as a stranger, the churches he took over were in deep debt and despair, and he started a university and a hospital with no capital. His only resources were his faith and his belief in a dream that would help others.

Family Sacrifices and Sorrows

Conwell admitted that he regretted not spending enough time with his family because of the great sacrifices he made to accomplish his goals. Fortunately, he had a very understanding and supportive wife who handled many of the duties and thus made it easier for her husband to excel in his life's work. Sarah Conwell was supportive to the point that she once agreed to give all of her possessions and allow Conwell to mortgage and sell all that he owned in order to help Temple University survive a financial crisis. She was probably one of the few women on the earth who had the understanding and temperament to have a harmonious marriage with a man as in-demand as Conwell was.

It was understandably a major blow for Conwell when his beloved wife passed away in 1910. Nine years prior, in 1901, he and Sarah had also suffered the agony of losing their daughter Agnes. Agnes was only twenty-six years old at the time of her death, and she was the only child from Conwell's second marriage.

One of his biographers noted that Conwell was a lonely man after the death of his second wife, also due to the fact that his other children had married and moved on, but he was not unhappy and did not have time to wallow in sadness because he kept so busy with his many obligations. Even in his last days, Conwell was a tireless worker who never took a lot of time off from his work. When he did take the time to rest, he often liked to go fishing because it was recreational and restful but also gave him time to think and plan. He even had a large pond, three-quarters of a mile long and half a mile wide, down a slope in front of his house where he could relax or go fishing. He also allowed many youngsters to come and fish for trout in his pond.

"Open the Gates of the Temple"

Conwell worked as much as possible until the very end. He kept an active schedule until failing health forced him to give up preaching and lecturing in May of 1925. Even as his health deteriorated in those final weeks, he charged certain staff members to continue the work he had started.

Because he was also somewhat burdened about leaving behind debt related to his work, a group of employees from the Philadelphia Rapid Transit Company gave a gift of $15,000 to pay the debt. This was a tremendous tribute to the impact that Conwell had on the common man.

On December 6, 1925, at 2:05 a.m., Russell Conwell breathed his last breath on earth and slipped into eternity at the age of eighty-two. Some of the final words his daughter heard him say were "the gates of the temple," letting her know that he wanted the choir to sing the hymn "Open the Gates of the Temple." He had fought a good fight on earth, and he had made life so much better for so many underprivileged people. Now, the great philanthropist was entering into the gates of the Temple to meet his glorious Maker.

At the going-home service for Conwell on Wednesday, December 9, his choir sang his favorite hymn, "Open the Gates of the Temple." The hymn contained a symbolism that Conwell loved because it signified a sincere sentiment for the place where thousands of individuals came to worship on a weekly basis—his church, "The Temple."

Those who paid tribute to Conwell at his funeral seemed to all point to the fact that he never really thought about himself but was always concerned about others. In a very fitting final tribute, Dr. William D. McCurdy, a man who had been Conwell's long-time associate, said this:

> The debt to Johnny Ring is paid now. The sword that the captain took from the parched hands of his orderly lies today in the captain's motionless hands. Two men's work has been done. This church and this university are monuments together to Doctor Conwell and Johnny Ring.

A Young Russell Conwell
in the Civil War

During his lifetime, Russell Conwell kept the sword hanging over his bed in his Philadelphia home to remind him of John Ring's tremendous sacrifice

Russell Conwell when he
entered the ministry at the
age of thirty-seven

The Baptist Temple was first occupied March 1, 1891

ACRES OF DIAMONDS

The World-Famous Lecture

By Russell H. Conwell

ACRES OF DIAMONDS

The following pages contain a note from Russell Conwell along with a complete form of his lecture from the book Acres of Diamonds (originally published in 1915 by Harper & Brothers). It happened to be delivered in Philadelphia, Dr. Conwell's home city. When he said, "Right here in Philadelphia," he meant the home city, town, or village of every reader of this book, just as he would have used the name of that town if he were delivering the lecture there. Please note that the lecture has been reprinted in its original form, so some of the figures of speech or spelling conventions will not conform to those of our present time.

A Note From Russell Conwell About This Lecture

Friends.—This lecture has been delivered under these circumstances: I visit a town or city, and try to arrive there early enough to see the postmaster, the barber, the keeper of the hotel, the principal of the schools, and the ministers of some of the churches, and then go into some of the factories and stores, and talk with the people, and get into sympathy with the local conditions of that town or city and see what has been their history, what opportunities they had, and what they had failed to do—and every town fails to do something—and then go to the lecture and talk to those people about the subjects which applied to their locality. "Acres of Diamonds"—the idea—has continually been precisely the same. The idea is that in this country of ours every man has the opportunity to make more of himself than he does in his own environment, with his own skill, with his own energy, and with his own friends.

RUSSELL H. CONWELL

ACRES OF DIAMONDS

When going down the Tigris and Euphrates rivers many years ago with a party of English travelers I found myself under the direction of an old Arab guide whom we hired up at Bagdad, and I have often thought how that guide resembled our barbers in certain mental characteristics. He thought that it was not only his duty to guide us down those rivers, and do what he was paid for doing, but also to entertain us with stories curious and weird, ancient and modern, strange and familiar. Many of them I have forgotten, and I am glad I have, but there is one I shall never forget.

The old guide was leading my camel by its halter along the banks of those ancient rivers, and he told me story after story until I grew weary of his story-telling and ceased to listen. I have never been irritated with that guide when he lost his temper as I ceased listening. But I remember that he took off his Turkish cap and swung it in a circle to get my attention. I could see it through the corner of my eye, but I determined not to look straight at him for fear he would tell another story. But although I am not a woman, I did finally look, and as soon as I did he went right into another story.

Said he, "I will tell you a story now which I reserve for my particular friends." When he emphasized the words "particular friends," I listened, and I have ever been glad I did. I really feel devoutly thankful, that there are 1,674 young men who have been carried through college by this lecture who are also glad that I did listen. The old guide told me that there once lived not far from the River Indus an ancient Persian by the name of Ali Hafed. He said that Ali Hafed owned a very large farm, that he had orchards, grain-fields, and gardens; that he had money at interest, and was a wealthy and contented man. He was contented because he was wealthy, and wealthy because he was contented. One day there visited that old Persian farmer one of these ancient Buddhist priests, one of the wise men of the East. He sat down by the fire and told the old farmer how this world of ours was made. He said that this world was once a mere bank of fog, and that the Almighty thrust His finger into this bank of fog, and began slowly to move His finger around, increasing the speed until at last He whirled this bank of fog into a solid ball of fire. Then it went rolling through the universe, burning its way through other banks of fog, and condensed the moisture without, until it fell in floods of rain upon its hot surface, and cooled the outward crust. Then the internal fires bursting outward through the crust threw up the mountains and hills, the valleys, the plains and prairies of this wonderful world of ours. If this internal molten mass came bursting out and cooled very quickly it became granite; less quickly copper, less quickly silver, less quickly gold, and, after gold, diamonds were made.

Said the old priest, "A diamond is a congealed drop of sunlight." Now that is literally scientifically true, that a diamond is an actual deposit of carbon from the sun. The old priest told Ali Hafed that if he had one diamond the size of his thumb he could purchase the county, and if he had a mine of diamonds he could place his children upon thrones through the influence of their great wealth.

ACRES OF DIAMONDS

Ali Hafed heard all about diamonds, how much they were worth, and went to his bed that night a poor man. He had not lost anything, but he was poor because he was discontented, and discontented because he feared he was poor. He said, "I want a mine of diamonds," and he lay awake all night.

Early in the morning he sought out the priest. I know by experience that a priest is very cross when awakened early in the morning, and when he shook that old priest out of his dreams, Ali Hafed said to him:

"Will you tell me where I can find diamonds?"

"Diamonds! What do you want with diamonds?" "Why, I wish to be immensely rich." "Well, then, go along and find them. That is all you have to do; go and find them, and then you have them" "But I don't know where to go." "Well, if you will find a river that runs through white sands, between high mountains, in those white sands you will always find diamonds." "I don't believe there is any such river." "Oh yes, there are plenty of them. All you have to do is to go and find them, and then you have them." Said Ali Hafed, "I will go."

So he sold his farm, collected his money, left his family in charge of a neighbor, and away he went in search of diamonds. He began his search, very properly to my mind, at the Mountains of the Moon. Afterward he came around into Palestine, then wandered on into Europe, and at last when his money was all spent and he was in rags, wretchedness, and poverty, he stood on the shore of that bay at Barcelona, in Spain, when a great tidal wave came rolling in between the pillars of Hercules, and the poor, afflicted, suffering, dying man could not resist the awful temptation to cast himself into that incoming tide, and he sank beneath its foaming crest, never to rise in this life again.

When that old guide had told me that awfully sad story he stopped the camel I was riding on and went back to fix the baggage that was coming off another camel, and I had an opportunity to muse over his story while he was gone. I remember saying to myself, "Why did he reserve that story for his 'particular friends'?" There seemed to be no beginning, no middle, no end, nothing to it. That was the first story I had ever heard told in my life, and would be the first one I ever read, in which the hero was killed in the first chapter. I had but one chapter of that story, and the hero was dead.

When the guide came back and took up the halter of my camel, he went right ahead with the story, into the second chapter, just as though there had been no break. The man who purchased Ali Hafed's farm one day led his camel into the garden to drink, and as that camel put its nose into the shallow water of that garden brook, Ali Hafed's successor noticed a curious flash of light from the white sands of the stream. He pulled out a black stone having an eye of light reflecting all the hues of the rainbow. He took the pebble into the house and put it on the mantel which covers the central fires, and forgot all about it.

A few days later this same old priest came in to visit Ali Hafed's successor, and the moment he opened that drawing-room door he saw that flash of light on the mantel, and he rushed up to it, and shouted: "Here is a diamond! Has Ali Hafed returned?" "Oh no, Ali Hafed has not returned, and that is not a diamond. That is nothing but a stone we found right out here in our own garden." "But," said the priest, "I tell you I know a diamond when I see it. I know positively that is a diamond."

Then together they rushed out into that old garden and stirred up the white sands with their fingers, and lo! there came up other more beautiful and valuable gems than the first. "Thus," said the guide to me, and, friends, it is historically true, "was discovered the diamond-mine of Golconda, the most magnificent diamond-mine in all the history of mankind, excelling the Kimberly itself. The Kohinoor, and the Orloff of the crown jewels of England and Russia, the largest on earth, came from that mine."

When that old Arab guide told me the second chapter of his story, he then took off his Turkish cap and swung it around in the air again to get my attention to the moral. Those Arab guides have morals to their stories, although they are not always moral. As he swung his hat, he said to me, "Had Ali Hafed remained at home and dug in his own cellar, or underneath his own wheat-fields, or in his own garden, instead of wretchedness, starvation, and death by suicide in a strange land, he would have had 'acres of diamonds.' For every acre of that old farm, yes, every shovelful, afterward revealed gems which since have decorated the crowns of monarchs."

When he had added the moral to his story I saw why he reserved it for "his particular friends." But I did not tell him I could see it. It was that mean old Arab's way of going around a thing like a lawyer, to say indirectly what he did not dare say directly, that "in his private opinion there was a certain young man then traveling down the Tigris River that might better be at home in America." I did not tell him I could see that, but I told him his story reminded me of one, and I told it to him quick, and I think I will tell it to you.

I told him of a man out in California in 1847 who owned a ranch. He heard they had discovered gold in southern California, and so with a passion for gold he sold his ranch to Colonel Sutter, and away he went, never to come back. Colonel Sutter put a mill upon a stream that ran through that ranch, and one day his little girl brought some wet sand from the raceway into their home and sifted it through her fingers before the fire, and in that falling sand a visitor saw the first shining scales of real gold that were ever discovered in California. The man who had owned that ranch wanted gold, and he could have secured it for the mere taking. Indeed, thirty-eight millions of dollars has been taken out of a very few acres since then. About eight years ago I delivered this lecture in a city that stands on that farm, and they told me that a one-third owner for years and years had been getting one hundred and twenty dollars in gold every fifteen minutes, sleeping or waking, without taxation. You and I would enjoy an income like that—if we didn't have to pay an income tax.

But a better illustration really than that occurred here in our own Pennsylvania. If there is anything I enjoy above another on the platform, it is to get one of these German audiences in Pennsylvania before me, and fire that at them, and I enjoy it to-night. There was a man living in Pennsylvania, not unlike some Pennsylvanians you have seen, who owned a farm, and he did with that farm just what I should do with a farm if I owned one in Pennsylvania—he sold it. But before he sold it he decided to secure employment collecting coal-oil for his cousin, who was in the business in Canada, where they first discovered oil on this continent. They dipped it from the running streams at that early time. So this Pennsylvania farmer wrote to his cousin asking for employment. You see, friends, this farmer was not altogether a foolish man. No, he was not. He did not leave his farm until he had something else to do. *Of all the simpletons the stars shine on I don't know of a worse one than the man who leaves one job before he has gotten another.* That has especial reference to my profession, and has no reference whatever to a man seeking a divorce. When he wrote to his cousin for employment, his cousin replied, "I cannot engage you because you know nothing about the oil business."

Well, then the old farmer said, "I will know," and with most commendable zeal (characteristic of the students of Temple University) he set himself at the study of the whole subject. He began away back at the second day of God's creation when this world was covered thick and deep with that rich vegetation which since has turned to the primitive beds of coal. He studied the subject until he found that the drainings really of those rich beds of coal furnished the coal-oil that was worth pumping, and then he found how it came up with the living springs. He studied until he knew what it looked like, smelled like, tasted like, and how to refine it. Now said he in his letter to his cousin, "I understand the oil business." His cousin answered, "All right, come on."

So he sold his farm, according to the county record, for $833 (even money, "no cents"). He had scarcely gone from that place before the man who purchased the spot went out to arrange for the watering of the cattle. He found the previous owner had gone out years before and put a plank across the brook back of the barn, edgewise into the surface of the water just a few inches. The purpose of that plank at that sharp angle across the brook was to throw over to the other bank a dreadful-looking scum through which the cattle would not put their noses. But with that plank there to throw it all over to one side, the cattle would drink below, and thus that man who had gone to Canada had been himself damming back for twenty-three years a flood of coal-oil which the state geologists of Pennsylvania declared to us ten years later was even then worth a hundred millions of dollars to our state, and four years ago our geologist declared the discovery to be worth to our state a thousand millions of dollars. The man who owned that territory on which the city of Titusville now stands, and those Pleasantville valleys, had studied the subject from the second day of God's creation clear down to the present time. He studied it until he knew all about it, and yet he is said to have sold the whole of it for $833, and again I say, "no sense."

But I need another illustration. I found it in Massachusetts, and I am sorry I did because that is the state I came from. This young man in Massachusetts furnishes just another phase of my thought. He went to Yale College and studied mines and mining, and became such an adept as a mining engineer that he was employed by the authorities of the university to train students who were behind their classes. During his senior year he earned $15 a week for doing that work. When he graduated they raised his pay from $15 to $45 a week, and offered him a professorship, and as soon as they did he went right home to his mother. *If they had raised that boy's pay from $15 to $15.60 he would have stayed and been proud of the place, but when they put it up to $45 at one leap, he said, "Mother, I won't work for $45 a week. The idea of a man with a brain like mine working for $45 a week!* Let's go out in California and stake out gold-mines and silver-mines, and be immensely rich."

Said his mother, "Now, Charlie, it is just as well to be happy as it is to be rich."

"Yes," said Charlie, "but it is just as well to be rich and happy, too." And they were both right about it. As he was an only son and she a widow, of course he had his way. They always do.

They sold out in Massachusetts, and instead of going to California they went to Wisconsin, where he went into the employ of the Superior Copper Mining Company at $15 a week again, but with the proviso in his contract that he should have an interest in any mines he should discover for the company. I don't believe he ever discovered a mine, and if I am looking in the face of any stockholder of that copper company you wish he had discovered something or other. I have friends who are not here because they could not afford a ticket, who did have stock in that company at the time this young man was employed there. This young man went out there, and I have not heard a word from him. I don't know what became of him, and I don't know whether he found any mines or not, but I don't believe he ever did.

But I do know the other end of the line. He had scarcely gotten out of the old homestead before the succeeding owner went out to dig potatoes. The potatoes were already growing in the ground when he bought the farm, and as the old farmer was bringing in a basket of potatoes it hugged very tight between the ends of the stone fence. You know in Massachusetts our farms are nearly all stone wall. There you are obliged to be very economical of front gateways in order to have some place to put the stone. When that basket hugged so tight he set it down on the ground, and then dragged on one side, and pulled on the other side, and as he was dragging that basket through this farmer noticed in the upper and outer corner of that stone wall, right next the gate, a block of native silver eight inches square. That professor of mines, mining, and mineralogy who knew so much about the subject that he would not work for $45 a week, when he sold that homestead in Massachusetts sat right on that silver to make the bargain. He was born on that homestead, was brought up there, and had gone back and forth rubbing the stone with his sleeve until it reflected his countenance, and seemed to say, "Here is a hundred thousand dollars right down here just for the taking." But he would not take it. It was in a home in Newburyport, Massachusetts, and there was no silver there, all away off—well, I don't know where, and he did not, but somewhere else, and he was a professor of mineralogy.

My friends, that mistake is very universally made, and why should we even smile at him. I often wonder what has become of him. I do not know at all, but I will tell you what I "guess" as a Yankee. I guess that he sits out there by his fireside to-night with his friends gathered around him, and he is saying to them something like this: "Do you know that man Conwell who lives in Philadelphia?" "Oh yes, I have heard of him." "Do you know that man Jones that lives in Philadelphia?" "Yes, I have heard of him, too."

Then he begins to laugh, and shakes his sides and says to his friends, "Well, they have done just the same thing I did, precisely"—and that spoils the whole joke, for you and I have done the same thing he did, and while we sit here and laugh at him he has a better right to sit out there and laugh at us. I know I have made the same mistakes, but, of course, that does not make any difference, because we don't expect the same man to preach and practise, too.

As I come here to-night and look around this audience I am seeing again what through these fifty years I have continually seen—men that are making precisely that same mistake. I often wish I could see the younger people, and would that the Academy had been filled to-night with our high-school scholars and our grammar-school scholars, that I could have them to talk to. While I would have preferred such an audience as that, because they are most susceptible, as they have not grown up into their prejudices as we have, they have not gotten into any custom that they cannot break, they have not met with any failures as we have; and while I could perhaps do such an audience as that more good than I can do grown-up people, yet I will do the best I can with the material I have. I say to you that you have "acres of diamonds" in Philadelphia right where you now live.

"Oh," but you will say, "you cannot know much about your city if you think there are any 'acres of diamonds' here."

I was greatly interested in that account in the newspaper of the young man who found that diamond in North Carolina. It was one of the purest diamonds that has ever been discovered, and it has several predecessors near the same locality. I went to a distinguished professor in mineralogy and asked him where he thought those diamonds came from. The professor secured the map of the geologic formations of our continent, and traced it. He said it went either through the underlying carboniferous strata adapted for such production, westward through Ohio and the Mississippi, or in more probability came eastward through Virginia and up the shore of the Atlantic Ocean. It is a fact that the diamonds were there, for they have been discovered and sold; and that they were carried down there during the drift period, from some northern locality. Now who can say but some person going down with his drill in Philadelphia will find some trace of a diamond-mine yet down here? Oh, friends! you cannot say that you are not over one of the greatest diamond-mines in the world, for such a diamond as that only comes from the most profitable mines that are found on earth.

> **Now then, I say again that the opportunity to get rich, to attain unto great wealth, is here in Philadelphia now, within the reach of almost every man and woman who hears me speak to-night, and I mean just what I say.**

But it serves simply to illustrate my thought, which I emphasize by saying if you do not have the actual diamond-mines literally you have all that they would be good for to you. Because now that the Queen of England has given the greatest compliment ever conferred upon American woman for her attire because she did not appear with any jewels at all at the late reception in England, it has almost done away with the use of diamonds anyhow. All you would care for would be the few you would wear if you wish to be modest, and the rest you would sell for money.

Now then, I say again that the opportunity to get rich, to attain unto great wealth, is here in Philadelphia now, within the reach of almost every man and woman who hears me speak to-night, and I mean just what I say. I have not come to this platform even under these circumstances to recite something to you. I have come to tell you what in God's sight I believe to be the truth, and if the years of life have been of any value to me in the attainment of common sense, I know I am right; that the men and women sitting here, who found it difficult perhaps to buy a ticket to this lecture or gathering to-night, have within their reach "acres of diamonds," opportunities to get largely wealthy. There never was a place on earth more adapted than the city of Philadelphia to-day, and never in the history of the world did a poor man without capital have such an opportunity to get rich quickly and honestly as he has now in our city. I say it is the truth, and I want you to accept it as such; for if you think I have come to simply recite something, then I would better not be here. I have no time to waste in any such talk, but to say the things I believe, and unless some of you get richer for what I am saying to-night my time is wasted.

I say that you ought to get rich, and it is your duty to get rich. How many of my pious brethren say to me, "Do you, a Christian minister, spend your time going up and down the country advising young people to get rich, to get money?" "Yes, of course I do." They say, "Isn't that awful! Why don't you preach the gospel instead of preaching about man's making money?" "Because to make money honestly is to preach the gospel." That is the reason. The men who get rich may be the most honest men you find in the community.

"Oh," but says some young man here to-night, "I have been told all my life that if a person has money he is very dishonest and dishonorable and mean and contemptible." My friend, that is the reason why you have none, because you have that idea of people. The foundation of your faith is altogether false. Let me say here clearly, and say it briefly, though subject to discussion which I have not time for here, ninety-eight out of one hundred of the rich men of America are honest. That is why they are rich. That is why they are trusted with money. That is why they carry on great enterprises and find plenty of people to work with them. It is because they are honest men.

Says another young man, "I hear sometimes of men that get millions of dollars dishonestly." Yes, of course you do, and so do I. But they are so rare a thing in fact that the newspapers talk about them all the time as a matter of news until you get the idea that all the other rich men got rich dishonestly.

My friend, you take and drive me—if you furnish the auto—out into the suburbs of Philadelphia, and introduce me to the people who own their homes around this great city, those beautiful homes with gardens and flowers, those magnificent homes so lovely in their art, and I will introduce you to the very best people in character as well as in enterprise in our city, and you know I will. A man is not really a true man until he owns his own home, and they that own their homes are made more honorable and honest and pure, and true and economical and careful, by owning the home.

For a man to have money, even in large sums, is not an inconsistent thing. We preach against covetousness, and you know we do, in the pulpit, and oftentimes preach against it so long and use the terms about "filthy lucre" so extremely that Christians get the idea that when we stand in the pulpit we believe it is wicked for any man to have money— until the collection-basket goes around, and then we almost swear at the people because they don't give more money. Oh, the inconsistency of such doctrines as that!

Money is power, and you ought to be reasonably ambitious to have it. You ought because you can do more good with it than you could without it. Money printed your Bible, money builds your churches, money sends your missionaries, and money pays your preachers, and you would not have many of them, either, if you did not pay them. I am always willing that my church should raise my salary, because the church that pays the largest salary always raises it the easiest. You never knew an exception to it in your life. The man who gets the largest salary can do the most good with the power that is furnished to him. Of course he can if his spirit be right to use it for what it is given to him.

I say, then, you ought to have money. If you can honestly attain unto riches in Philadelphia, it is your Christian and godly duty to do so. It is an awful mistake of these pious people to think you must be awfully poor in order to be pious.

Some men say, "Don't you sympathize with the poor people?" Of course I do, or else I would not have been lecturing these years. I won't give in but what I sympathize with the poor, but the number of poor who are to be sympathized with is very small. To sympathize with a man whom God has punished for his sins, thus to help him when God would still continue a just punishment, is to do wrong, no doubt about it, and we do that more than we help those who are deserving. While we should sympathize with God's poor—that is, those who cannot help themselves—let us remember there is not a poor person in the United States who was not made poor by his own shortcomings, or by the shortcomings of some one else. It is all wrong to be poor, anyhow. Let us give in to that argument and pass that to one side.

A gentleman gets up back there, and says, "Don't you think there are some things in this world that are better than money?" Of course I do, but I am talking about money now. Of course there are some things higher than money. Oh yes, I know by the grave that has left me standing alone that there are some things in this world that are higher and sweeter and purer than money. Well do I know there are some things higher and grander than gold. Love is the grandest thing on God's earth, but fortunate the lover who has plenty of money. Money is power, money is force, money will do good as well as harm. In the hands of good men and women it could accomplish, and it has accomplished, good.

I hate to leave that behind me. I heard a man get up in a prayer-meeting in our city and thank the Lord he was "one of God's poor." Well, I wonder what his wife thinks about that? She earns all the money that comes into that house, and he smokes a part of

> **I heard a man get up in a prayer-meeting in our city and thank the Lord he was "one of God's poor." Well, I wonder what his wife thinks about that? She earns all the money that comes into that house, and he smokes a part of that on the veranda. I don't want to see any more of the Lord's poor of that kind, and I don't believe the Lord does. And yet there are some people who think in order to be pious you must be awfully poor and awfully dirty. That does not follow at all. While we sympathize with the poor, let us not teach a doctrine like that.**

that on the veranda. I don't want to see any more of the Lord's poor of that kind, and I don't believe the Lord does. And yet there are some people who think in order to be pious you must be awfully poor and awfully dirty. That does not follow at all. While we sympathize with the poor, let us not teach a doctrine like that.

Yet the age is prejudiced against advising a Christian man (or, as a Jew would say, a godly man) from attaining unto wealth. The prejudice is so universal and the years are far enough back, I think, for me to safely mention that years ago up at Temple University there was a young man in our theological school who thought he was the only pious student in that department. He came into my office one evening and sat down by my desk, and said to me: "Mr. President, I think it is my duty sir, to come in and labor with you." "What has happened now?" Said he, "I heard you say at the Academy, at the Peirce School commencement, that you thought it was an honorable ambition for a young man to desire to have wealth, and that you thought it made him temperate, made him anxious to have a good name, and made him industrious. You spoke about man's ambition to have money helping to make him a good man. Sir, I have come to tell you the Holy Bible says that 'money is the root of all evil.'"

I told him I had never seen it in the Bible, and advised him to go out into the chapel and get the Bible, and show me the place. So out he went for the Bible, and soon he stalked into my office with the Bible open, with all the bigoted pride of the narrow sectarian, or of one who founds his Christianity on some misinterpretation of Scripture. He flung the Bible down on my desk, and fairly squealed into my ear: "There it is, Mr. President; you can read it for yourself." I said to him: "Well, young man, you will learn when you get a little older that you cannot trust another denomination to read the Bible for you. You belong to another denomination. You are taught in the theological school, however, that emphasis is exegesis. Now, will you take that Bible and read it yourself, and give the proper emphasis to it?"

He took the Bible, and proudly read, " 'The love of money is the root of all evil.' "

Then he had it right, and when one does quote aright from that same old Book he quotes the absolute truth. I have lived through fifty years of the mightiest battle that old Book has ever fought, and I have lived to see its banners flying free; for never in the history of this world did the great minds of earth so universally agree that the Bible is true—all true—as they do at this very hour.

> **The love of money. What is that? It is making an idol of money, and idolatry pure and simple everywhere is condemned by the Holy Scriptures and by man's common sense. The man that worships the dollar instead of thinking of the purposes for which it ought to be used, the man who idolizes simply money, the miser that hordes his money in the cellar, or hides it in his stocking, or refuses to invest it where it will do the world good, that man who hugs the dollar until the eagle squeals has in him the root of all evil.**

So I say that when he quoted right, of course he quoted the absolute truth. "The love of money is the root of all evil." He who tries to attain unto it too quickly, or dishonestly, will fall into many snares, no doubt about that. The love of money. What is that? It is making an idol of money, and idolatry pure and simple everywhere is condemned by the Holy Scriptures and by man's common sense. The man that worships the dollar instead of thinking of the purposes for which it ought to be used, the man who idolizes simply money, the miser that hordes his money in the cellar, or hides it in his stocking, or refuses to invest it where it will do the world good, that man who hugs the dollar until the eagle squeals has in him the root of all evil.

I think I will leave that behind me now and answer the question of nearly all of you who are asking, "Is there opportunity to get rich in Philadelphia?" Well, now, how simple a thing it is to see where it is, and the instant you see where it is it is yours. Some old gentleman gets up back there and says, "Mr. Conwell, have you lived in Philadelphia for thirty-one years and don't know that the time has gone by when you can make anything in this city?" "No, I don't think it is." "Yes, it is; I have tried it." "What business are you in?" "I kept a store here for twenty years, and never made over a thousand dollars in the whole twenty years."

"Well, then, you can measure the good you have been to this city by what this city has paid you, because a man can judge very well what he is worth by what he receives; that is, in what he is to the world at this time. If you have not made over a thousand dollars in twenty years in Philadelphia, it would have been better for Philadelphia if they had kicked you out of the city nineteen years and nine months ago. A man has no right to keep a store in Philadelphia twenty years and not make at least five hundred thousand dollars even though it be a corner grocery up-town." You say, "You cannot make five thousand dollars in a store now." Oh, my friends, if you will just take only four blocks around you, and find out what the people want and what you ought to supply and set them down with your pencil and figure up the profits you would make if you did supply them, you would very soon see it. There is wealth right within the sound of your voice.

Some one says: "You don't know anything about business. A preacher never knows a thing about business." Well, then, I will have to prove that I am an expert. I don't like to do this, but I have to do it because my testimony will not be taken if I am not an expert. My father kept a country store, and if there is any place under the stars where a man gets all sorts of experience in every kind of mercantile transactions, it is in the country store. I am not proud of my experience, but sometimes when my father was away he would leave me in charge of the store, though fortunately for him that was not very often. But this did occur many times, friends: A man would come in the store, and say to me, "Do you keep jack-knives?" "No, we don't keep jack-knives," and I went off whistling a tune. What did I care about that man, anyhow? Then another farmer would come in and say, "Do you keep jack-knives?" "No, we don't keep jack-knives." Then I went away and whistled another tune. Then a third man came right in the same door and said, "Do you keep jack-knives?" "No. Why is every one around here asking for jack-knives? Do you suppose we are keeping this store to supply the whole neighborhood with jack-knives?" Do you carry on your store like that in Philadelphia? The difficulty was I had not then learned that the foundation of godliness and the foundation principle of success in business are both the same precisely. The man who says, "I cannot carry my religion into business" advertises himself either as being an imbecile in business, or on the road to bankruptcy, or a thief, one of the three, sure. He will fail within a very few years. He certainly will if he doesn't carry his religion into business. If I had been carrying on my father's store on a Christian plan, godly plan, I would have had a jack-knife for the third man when he called for it. Then I would have actually done him a kindness, and I would have received a reward myself, which it would have been my duty to take.

There are some over-pious Christian people who think if you take any profit on anything you sell that you are an unrighteous man. On the contrary, you would be a criminal to sell goods for less than they cost. You have no right to do that. You cannot trust a man with your money who cannot take care of his own. You cannot trust a man in your family that is not true to his own wife. You cannot trust a man in the world that does not begin with his own heart, his own character, and his own life. It would have been my duty to have furnished a jack-knife to the third man, or the second, and to have sold it to him and actually profited myself. I have no more right to sell goods without making a profit on them than I have to overcharge him dishonestly beyond what they are worth. But I should so sell each bill of goods that the person to whom I sell shall make as much as I make.

To live and let live is the principle of the gospel, and the principle of every-day common sense. Oh, young man, hear me; live as you go along. Do not wait until you have reached my years before you begin to enjoy anything of this life. If I had the millions back, or fifty cents of it, which I have tried to earn in these years, it would not do me anything like the good that it does me now in this almost sacred presence to-night. Oh, yes, I am paid over and over a hundredfold to-night for dividing as I have tried to do in some measure as I went along through the years. I ought not speak that way, it sounds egotistic, but I am old enough now to be excused for that. I should have helped my fellow-men, which I have tried to do, and every one should try to do, and get the happiness of it. The man who goes home with the sense that he has stolen a dollar that day, that he has robbed a man of what was his honest due, is not going to sweet rest. He arises tired in the morning, and goes with an unclean conscience to his work the next day. He is not a successful man at all, although he may have laid up millions. But the man who has gone through life dividing always with his fellow-men, making and demanding his own rights and his own profits, and giving to every other man his rights and profits, lives every day, and not only that, but it is the royal road to great wealth. The history of the thousands of millionaires shows that to be the case.

> ## "Oh, if I had plenty of capital, how rich I would get." "Young man, do you think you are going to get rich on capital?" "Certainly." Well, I say, "Certainly not."

The man over there who said he could not make anything in a store in Philadelphia has been carrying on his store on the wrong principle. Suppose I go into your store to-morrow morning and ask, "Do you know neighbor A, who lives one square away, at house No. 1240?" "Oh yes, I have met him. He deals here at the corner store." "Where did he come from?" "I don't know." "How many does he have in his family?" "I don't know." "What ticket does he vote?" "I don't know." "What church does he go to?" "I don't know, and don't care. What are you asking all these questions for?"

If you had a store in Philadelphia would you answer me like that? If so, then you are conducting your business just as I carried on my father's business in Worthington, Massachusetts. You don't know where your neighbor came from when he moved to Philadelphia, and you don't care. If you had cared you would be a rich man now. If you had cared enough about him to take an interest in his affairs, to find out what he needed, you would have been rich. But you go through the world saying, "No opportunity to get rich," and there is the fault right at your own door.

But another young man gets up over there and says, "I cannot take up the mercantile business." (While I am talking of trade it applies to every occupation.) "Why can't you go into the mercantile business?" "Because I haven't any capital." Oh, the weak and dudish creature that can't see over its collar! It makes a person weak to see these little dudes standing around the corners and saying, "Oh, if I had plenty of capital, how rich I would get." "Young man, do you think you are going to get rich on capital?" "Certainly." Well, I say, "Certainly not." If your mother has plenty of money, and she will set you up in business, you will "set her up in business," supplying you with capital.

ACRES OF DIAMONDS

The moment a young man or woman gets more money than he or she has grown to by practical experience, that moment he has gotten a curse. It is no help to a young man or woman to inherit money. It is no help to your children to leave them money, but if you leave them education, if you leave them Christian and noble character, if you leave them a wide circle of friends, if you leave them an honorable name, it is far better than that they should have money. It would be worse for them, worse for the nation, that they should have any money at all. Oh, young man, if you have inherited money, don't regard it as a help. It will curse you through your years, and deprive you of the very best things of human life. There is no class of people to be pitied so much as the inexperienced sons and daughters of the rich of our generation. I pity the rich man's son. He can never know the best things in life.

One of the best things in our life is when a young man has earned his own living, and when he becomes engaged to some lovely young woman, and makes up his mind to have a home of his own. Then with that same love comes also that divine inspiration toward better things, and he begins to save his money. He begins to leave off his bad habits and put money in the bank. When he has a few hundred dollars he goes out in the suburbs to look for a home. He goes to the savings-bank, perhaps, for half of the value,

---

The moment a young man or woman gets more money than he or she has grown to by practical experience, that moment he has gotten a curse. It is no help to a young man or woman to inherit money. It is no help to your children to leave them money, but if you leave them education, if you leave them Christian and noble character, if you leave them a wide circle of friends, if you leave them an honorable name, it is far better than that they should have money.

---

and then goes for his wife, and when he takes his bride over the threshold of that door for the first time he says in words of eloquence my voice can never touch: "I have earned this home myself. It is all mine, and I divide with thee." That is the grandest moment a human heart may ever know.

But a rich man's son can never know that. He takes his bride into a finer mansion, it may be, but he is obliged to go all the way through it and say to his wife, "My mother gave me that, my mother gave me that, and my mother gave me this," until his wife wishes she had married his mother. I pity the rich man's son.

The statistics of Massachusetts showed that not one rich man's son out of seventeen ever dies rich. I pity the rich man's sons unless they have the good sense of the elder Vanderbilt, which sometimes happens. He went to his father and said, "Did you earn all your money?" "I did, my son. I began to work on a ferry-boat for twenty-five cents a day." "Then," said his son, "I will have none of your money," and he, too, tried to get employment on a ferry-boat that Saturday night. He could not get one there, but he did get a place for three dollars a week. Of course, if a rich man's son will do that, he will get the discipline of a poor boy that is worth more than a university education to any man. He would then be able to take care of the millions of his father. But as a rule the rich men will not let their sons do the very thing that made them great. As a rule, the rich man will not allow his son to work—and his mother! Why, she would think it was a social disgrace if her poor, weak, little lily-fingered, sissy sort of a boy had to earn his living with honest toil. I have no pity for such rich men's sons.

I remember one at Niagara Falls. I think I remember one a great deal nearer. I think there are gentlemen present who were at a great banquet, and I beg pardon of his friends. At a banquet here in Philadelphia there sat beside me a kind-hearted young man, and he said, "Mr. Conwell, you have been sick for two or three years. When you go out, take my limousine, and it will take you up to your house on Broad Street." I thanked him very much, and perhaps I ought not to mention the incident in this way, but I follow the facts. I got on to the seat with the driver of that limousine, outside, and when we were going up I asked the driver, "How much did this limousine cost?" "Six thousand eight hundred, and he had to pay the duty on it." "Well," I said, "does the owner of this machine ever drive it himself?" At that the chauffeur laughed so heartily that he lost control of his

> **Of course, if a rich man's son will do that, he will get the discipline of a poor boy that is worth more than a university education to any man. He would then be able to take care of the millions of his father. But as a rule the rich men will not let their sons do the very thing that made them great. As a rule, the rich man will not allow his son to work—and his mother! Why, she would think it was a social disgrace if her poor, weak, little lily-fingered, sissy sort of a boy had to earn his living with honest toil. I have no pity for such rich men's sons.**

machine. He was so surprised at the question that he ran up on the sidewalk, and around a corner lamp-post out into the street again. And when he got out into the street he laughed till the whole machine trembled. He said: "He drive this machine! Oh, he would be lucky if he knew enough to get out when we get there."

I must tell you about a rich man's son at Niagara Falls. I came in from the lecture to the hotel, and as I approached the desk of the clerk there stood a millionaire's son from New York. He was an indescribable specimen of anthropologic potency. He had a skull-cap on one side of his head, with a gold tassel in the top of it, and a gold-headed cane under his arm with more in it than in his head. It is a very difficult thing to describe that young man. He wore an eye-glass that he could not see through, patent-leather boots that he could not walk in, and pants that he could not sit down in—dressed like a grasshopper. This human cricket came up to the clerk's desk just as I entered, adjusted his unseeing eye-glass, and spake in this wise to the clerk. You see, he thought it was "Hinglish, you know," to lisp. "Thir, will you have the kindness to supply me with thome papah and enwelophs!" The hotel clerk measured that man quick, and he pulled the envelopes and paper out of a drawer, threw them across the counter toward the young man, and then turned away to his books. You should have seen that young man when those envelopes came across that counter. He swelled up like a gobbler turkey, adjusted his unseeing eye-glass, and yelled: "Come right back here. Now thir, will you order a thervant to take that papah and enwelophs to yondah dethk." Oh, the poor, miserable, contemptible American monkey! He could not carry paper and envelopes twenty feet. I suppose he could not get his arms down to do it. I have no pity for such travesties upon human nature. If you have not capital, young man, I am glad of it. What you need is common sense, not copper cents.

The best thing I can do is to illustrate by actual facts well-known to you all. A. T. Stewart, a poor boy in New York, had $1.50 to begin life on. He lost 87 1/2 cents of that on the very first venture. How fortunate that young man who loses the first time he gambles. That boy said, "I will never gamble again in business," and he never did. How came he to lose 87 1/2 cents? You probably all know the story how he lost it—because he bought some needles, threads, and buttons to sell which people did not want, and had

---

Study it wherever you choose—in business, in your profession, in your housekeeping, whatever your life, that one thing is the secret of success. You must first know the demand. You must first know what people need, and then invest yourself where you are most needed. A. T. Stewart went on that principle until he was worth what amounted afterward to forty millions of dollars, owning the very store in which Mr. Wanamaker carries on his great work in New York.

---

them left on his hands, a dead loss. Said the boy, "I will not lose any more money in that way." Then he went around first to the doors and asked the people what they did want. Then when he had found out what they wanted he invested his 62 1/2 cents to supply a known demand. Study it wherever you choose—in business, in your profession, in your housekeeping, whatever your life, that one thing is the secret of success. You must first know the demand. You must first know what people need, and then invest yourself where you are most needed. A. T. Stewart went on that principle until he was worth what amounted afterward to forty millions of dollars, owning the very store in which Mr. Wanamaker carries on his great work in New York. His fortune was made by his losing something, which taught him the great lesson that he must only invest himself or his money in something that people need. When will you salesmen learn it? When will you manufacturers learn that you must know the changing needs of humanity if you would succeed in life? Apply yourselves, all you Christian people, as manufacturers or mer-chants or workmen to supply that human need. It is a great principle as broad as human-ity and as deep as the Scripture itself.

The best illustration I ever heard was of John Jacob Astor. You know that he made the money of the Astor family when he lived in New York. He came across the sea in debt for his fare. But that poor boy with nothing in his pocket made the fortune of the Astor family on one principle. Some young man here to-night will say, "Well they could make those fortunes over in New York but they could not do it in Philadelphia!" My friends, did you ever read that wonderful book of Riis (his memory is sweet to us because of his recent death), wherein is given his statistical account of the records taken in 1889 of 107 millionaires of New York. If you read the account you will see that out of the 107 millionaires only seven made their money in New York. Out of the 107 millionaires worth ten million dollars in real estate then, 67 of them made their money in towns of less than 3,500 inhabitants. The richest man in this country to-day, if you read the real-estate values, has never moved away from a town of 3,500 inhabitants. It makes not so much difference where you are as who you are. But if you cannot get rich in Philadelphia you certainly cannot do it in New York.

Now John Jacob Astor illustrated what can be done anywhere. He had a mortgage once on a millinery-store, and they could not sell bonnets enough to pay the interest on his money. So he foreclosed that mortgage, took possession of the store, and went into partnership with the very same people, in the same store, with the same capital. He did not give them a dollar of capital. They had to sell goods to get any money. Then he left them alone in the store just as they had been before, and he went out and sat down on a

---

It makes not so much difference where you are as who you are. But if you cannot get rich in Philadelphia you certainly cannot do it in New York.

---

bench in the park in the shade. What was John Jacob Astor doing out there, and in partnership with people who had failed on his own hands? He had the most important and, to my mind, the most pleasant part of that partnership on his hands. For as John Jacob Astor sat on that bench he was watching the ladies as they went by; and where is the man who would not get rich at that business? As he sat on the bench if a lady passed him with her shoulders back and head up, and looked straight to the front, as if she did not care if all the world did gaze on her, then he studied her bonnet, and by the time it was out of sight he knew the shape of the frame, the color of the trimmings, and the crinklings in the feather. I sometimes try to describe a bonnet, but not always. I would not try to describe a modern bonnet. Where is the man that could describe one? This aggregation of all sorts of driftwood stuck on the back of the head, or the side of the neck, like a rooster with only one tail feather left. But in John Jacob Astor's day there was some art about the millinery business, and he went to the millinery-store and said to them: "Now put into the show-window just such a bonnet as I describe to you, because I have already seen a lady who likes such a bonnet. Don't make up any more until I come back." Then he went out and sat down again, and another lady passed him of a different form, of different complexion, with a different shape and color of bonnet. "Now," said he, "put such a bonnet as that in the show window." He did not fill his show-window up town with a lot of hats and bonnets to drive people away, and then sit on the back stairs and bawl because people went to Wanamaker's to trade. He did not have a hat or a bonnet in that show-window but what some lady liked before it was made up. The tide of custom began immediately to turn in, and that has been the foundation of the greatest store in New York in that line, and still exists as one of three stores. Its fortune was made by John Jacob Astor after they had failed in business, not by giving them any more money, but by finding out what the ladies liked for bonnets before they wasted any material in making them up. I tell you if a man could foresee the millinery business he could foresee anything under heaven!

Suppose I were to go through this audience to-night and ask you in this great manufacturing city if there are not opportunities to get rich in manufacturing. "Oh yes," some young man says, "there are opportunities here still if you build with some trust and if you have two or three millions of dollars to begin with as capital." Young man, the history of the breaking up of the trusts by that attack upon "big business" is only illustrating what is now the opportunity of the smaller man. The time never came in the history of the world when you could get rich so quickly manufacturing without capital as you can now.

But you will say, "You cannot do anything of the kind. You cannot start without capital." Young man, let me illustrate for a moment. I must do it. It is my duty to every young man and woman, because we are all going into business very soon on the same plan. Young man, remember if you know what people need you have gotten more knowledge of a fortune than any amount of capital can give you.

There was a poor man out of work living in Hingham, Massachusetts. He lounged around the house until one day his wife told him to get out and work, and, as he lived in Massachusetts, he obeyed his wife. He went out and sat down on the shore of the bay, and whittled a soaked shingle into a wooden chain. His children that evening quarreled over it, and he whittled a second one to keep peace. While he was whittling the second one a neighbor came in and said: "Why don't you whittle toys and sell them? You could make money at that." "Oh," he said, "I would not know what to make." "Why don't you ask your own children right here in your own house what to make?" "What is the use of trying that?" said the carpenter. "My children are different from other people's children." (I used to see people like that when I taught school.) But he acted upon the hint, and the next morning when Mary came down the stairway, he asked, "What do you want for a toy?" She began to tell him she would like a doll's bed, a doll's washstand, a doll's carriage, a little doll's umbrella, and went on with a list of things that would take him a lifetime to supply. So, consulting his own children, in his own house, he took the firewood, for he had no money to buy lumber, and whittled those strong, unpainted Hingham toys that were for so many years known all over the world. That man began to make those toys for his own children, and then made copies and sold them through the boot-and-shoe store next door. He began to make a little money, and then a little more, and Mr. Lawson, in his *Frenzied Finance* says that man is the richest man in old Massachusetts, and I think it is the truth. And that man is worth a hundred millions of dollars to-day, and has been only thirty-four years making it on that one principle—that one must judge that what his own children like at home other people's children would like in their homes, too; to judge the human heart by oneself, by one's wife or by one's children. It is the royal road to success in manufacturing. "Oh," but you say, "didn't he have any capital?" Yes, a penknife, but I don't know that he had paid for that.

I spoke thus to an audience in New Britain, Connecticut, and a lady four seats back went home and tried to take off her collar, and the collar-button stuck in the buttonhole. She threw it out and said, "I am going to get up something better than that to put on collars." Her husband said: "After what Conwell said to-night, you see there is a need of an improved collar-fastener that is easier to handle. There is a human need; there is a great fortune. Now, then, get up a collar-button and get rich." He made fun of her, and consequently made fun of me, and that is one of the saddest things which comes over me like a deep cloud of midnight sometimes—although I have worked so hard for more than half a century, yet how little I have ever really done. Notwithstanding the greatness and the handsomeness of your compliment to-night, I do not believe there is one in ten of you that is going to make a million of dollars because you are here to-night; but it is not my fault, it is yours. I say that sincerely. What is the use of my talking if people never do what I advise them to do? When her husband ridiculed her, she made up her mind she would make a better collar-button, and when a woman makes up her mind "she will," and does not say anything about it, she does it. It was that New England woman who invented the snap button which you can find anywhere now. It was first a collar-button with a spring cap attached to the outer side. Any of you who wear modern waterproofs know the button that simply pushes together, and when you unbutton it you simply pull it apart. That is the button to which I refer, and which she invented. She afterward invented several other buttons, and then invested in more, and then was taken into partnership with great factories. Now that woman goes over the sea every summer in her private steamship—yes, and takes her husband with her! If her husband were to die, she would have money enough left now to buy a foreign duke or count or some such title as that at the latest quotations.

Now what is my lesson in that incident? It is this: I told her then, though I did not know her, what I now say to you, "Your wealth is too near to you. You are looking right over it"; and she had to look over it because it was right under her chin.

I have read in the newspaper that a woman never invented anything. Well, that newspaper ought to begin again. Of course, I do not refer to gossip—I refer to machines—and if I did I might better include the men. That newspaper could never appear if women had not invented something. Friends, think. Ye women, think! You say you cannot make a fortune because you are in some laundry, or running a sewing-machine, it may be, or walking before some loom, and yet you can be a millionaire if you will but follow this almost infallible direction.

When you say a woman doesn't invent anything, I ask, Who invented the Jacquard loom that wove every stitch you wear? Mrs. Jacquard. The printer's roller, the printing-press, were invented by farmers' wives. Who invented the cotton-gin of the South that enriched our country so amazingly? Mrs. General Greene invented the cotton-gin and showed the idea to Mr. Whitney, and he, like a man, seized it. Who was it that invented the sewing-machine? If I would go to school to-morrow and ask your children they would say, "Elias Howe."

He was in the Civil War with me, and often in my tent, and I often heard him say that he worked fourteen years to get up that sewing-machine. But his wife made up her mind one day that they would starve to death if there wasn't something or other invented pretty soon, and so in two hours she invented the sewing-machine. Of course he took out the patent in his name. Men always do that. Who was it that invented the mower and the reaper? According to Mr. McCormick's confidential communication, so recently published, it was a West Virginia woman, who, after his father and he had failed altogether in making a reaper and gave it up, took a lot of shears and nailed them together on the edge of a board, with one shaft of each pair loose, and then wired them so that when she pulled the wire one way it closed them, and when she pulled the wire the other way it opened them, and there she had the principle of the mowing-machine. If you look at a mowing-machine, you will see it is nothing but a lot of shears. If a woman can invent a mowing-machine, if a woman can invent a Jacquard loom, if a woman can invent a cotton-gin, if a woman can invent a trolley switch—as she did and made the trolleys possible; if a woman can invent, as Mr. Carnegie said, the great iron squeezers that laid the foundation of all the steel millions of the United States, "we men" can invent anything under the stars! I say that for the encouragement of the men.

Who are the great inventors of the world? Again this lesson comes before us. The great inventor sits next to you, or you are the person yourself. "Oh," but you will say, "I have never invented anything in my life." Neither did the great inventors until they discovered one great secret. Do you think it is a man with a head like a bushel measure or a man like a stroke of lightning? It is neither. The really great man is a plain, straightforward, every-day, common-sense man. You would not dream that he was a great inventor if you did not see something he had actually done. His neighbors do not regard him so great. You never see anything great over your back fence. You say there is no greatness among your neighbors. It is all away off somewhere else. Their greatness is ever so sim-

> **"Oh," but you will say, "I have never invented anything in my life." Neither did the great inventors until they discovered one great secret.**

ple, so plain, so earnest, so practical, that the neighbors and friends never recognize it.

True greatness is often unrecognized. That is sure. You do not know anything about the greatest men and women. I went out to write the life of General Garfield, and a neighbor, knowing I was in a hurry, and as there was a great crowd around the front door, took me around to General Garfield's back door and shouted, "Jim! Jim!" And very soon "Jim" came to the door and let me in, and I wrote the biography of one of the grandest men of the nation, and yet he was just the same old "Jim" to his neighbor. If you know a great man in Philadelphia and you should meet him to-morrow, you would say, "How are you, Sam?" or "Good morning, Jim." Of course you would. That is just what you would do.

One of my soldiers in the Civil War had been sentenced to death, and I went up to the White House in Washington—sent there for the first time in my life—to see the President. I went into the waiting-room and sat down with a lot of others on the benches, and the secretary asked one after another to tell him what they wanted. After the secretary had been through the line, he went in, and then came back to the door and motioned for me. I went up to that anteroom, and the secretary said: "That is the President's door right over there. Just rap on it and go right in." I never was so taken aback, friends, in all my life, never. The secretary himself made it worse for me, because he had told me how to go in and then went out another door to the left and shut that. There I was, in the hallway by myself before the President of the United States of America's door. I had been on fields of battle, where the shells did sometimes shriek and the bullets did sometimes hit me, but I always wanted to run. I have no sympathy with the old man who says, "I would just as soon march up to the cannon's mouth as eat my dinner." I have no faith in a man who doesn't know enough to be afraid when he is being shot at. I never was so afraid when the shells came around us at Antietam as I was when I went into that room that day; but I finally mustered the courage—I don't know how I ever did—and at arm's-length tapped on the door. The man inside did not help me at all, but yelled out, "Come in and sit down!"

Well, I went in and sat down on the edge of a chair, and wished I were in Europe, and the man at the table did not look up. He was one of the world's greatest men, and was made great by one single rule. Oh, that all the young people of Philadelphia were before me now and I could say just this one thing, and that they would remember it. I would give a lifetime for the effect it would have on our city and on civilization. Abraham Lincoln's principle for greatness can be adopted by nearly all. This was his rule: Whatsoever he had to do at all, he put his whole mind into it and held it all there until that was all done. That makes men great almost anywhere. He stuck to those papers at that table and did not look up at me, and I sat there trembling. Finally, when he had put

> **Abraham Lincoln's principle for greatness can be adopted by nearly all. This was his rule: Whatsoever he had to do at all, he put his whole mind into it and held it all there until that was all done. That makes men great almost anywhere. He stuck to those papers at that table and did not look up at me, and I sat there trembling.**

the string around his papers, he pushed them over to one side and looked over to me, and a smile came over his worn face. He said: "I am a very busy man and have only a few minutes to spare. Now tell me in the fewest words what it is you want." I began to tell him, and mentioned the case, and he said: "I have heard all about it and you do not need to say any more. Mr. Stanton was talking to me only a few days ago about that. You can go to the hotel and rest assured that the President never did sign an order to shoot a boy under twenty years of age, and never will. You can say that to his mother anyhow."

Then he said to me, "How is it going in the field?" I said, "We sometimes get discouraged." And he said: "It is all right. We are going to win out now. We are getting very near the light. No man ought to wish to be President of the United States, and I will be glad when I get through; then Tad and I are going out to Springfield, Illinois. I have bought a farm out there and I don't care if I again earn only twenty-five cents a day. Tad has a mule team, and we are going to plant onions."

Then he asked me, "Were you brought up on a farm?" I said, "Yes; in the Berkshire Hills of Massachusetts." He then threw his leg over the corner of the big chair and said, "I have heard many a time, ever since I was young, that up there in those hills you have to sharpen the noses of the sheep in order to get down to the grass between the rocks." He was so familiar, so everyday, so farmer-like, that I felt right at home with him at once.

He then took hold of another roll of paper, and looked up at me and said, "Good morning." I took the hint then and got up and went out. After I had gotten out I could not realize I had seen the President of the United States at all. But a few days later, when still in the city, I saw the crowd pass through the East Room by the coffin of Abraham Lincoln, and when I looked at the upturned face of the murdered President I felt then that the man I had seen such a short time before, who, so simple a man, so plain a man, was one of the greatest men that God ever raised up to lead a nation on to ultimate liberty. Yet he was only "Old Abe" to his neighbors. When they had the second funeral, I was invited among others, and went out to see that same coffin put back in the tomb at Springfield. Around the tomb stood Lincoln's old neighbors, to whom he was just "Old Abe." Of course that is all they would say.

Did you ever see a man who struts around altogether too large to notice an ordinary working mechanic? Do you think he is great? He is nothing but a puffed-up balloon, held down by his big feet. There is no greatness there.

Who are the great men and women? My attention was called the other day to the history of a very little thing that made the fortune of a very poor man. It was an awful thing, and yet because of that experience he—not a great inventor or genius—invented the pin that now is called the safety-pin, and out of that safety-pin made the fortune of one of the great aristocratic families of this nation.

A poor man in Massachusetts who had worked in the nail-works was injured at

> **Did you ever see a man who struts around altogether too large to notice an ordinary working mechanic? Do you think he is great? He is nothing but a puffed-up balloon, held down by his big feet. There is no greatness there.**

thirty-eight, and he could earn but little money. He was employed in the office to rub out the marks on the bills made by pencil memorandums, and he used a rubber until his hand grew tired. He then tied a piece of rubber on the end of a stick and worked it like a plane. His little girl came and said, "Why, you have a patent, haven't you?" The father said afterward, "My daughter told me when I took that stick and put the rubber on the end that there was a patent, and that was the first thought of that." He went to Boston and applied for his patent, and every one of you that has a rubber-tipped pencil in your pocket is now paying tribute to the millionaire. No capital, not a penny did he invest in it. All was income, all the way up into the millions.

But let me hasten to one other greater thought. "Show me the great men and women who live in Philadelphia." A gentleman over there will get up and say: "We don't have any great men in Philadelphia. They don't live here. They live away off in Rome or St. Petersburg or London or Manayunk, or anywhere else but here in our town." I have come now to the apex of my thought. I have come now to the heart of the whole matter and to the center of my struggle: Why isn't Philadelphia a greater city in its greater wealth? Why does New York excel Philadelphia? People say, "Because of her harbor." Why do many other cities of the United States get ahead of Philadelphia now? There is only one answer, and that is because our own people talk down their own city. If there ever was a community on earth that has to be forced ahead, it is the city of Philadelphia. If we are to have a boulevard, talk it down; if we are going to have better schools, talk them down; if you wish to have wise legislation, talk it down; talk all the proposed improvements down. That is the only great wrong that I can lay at the feet of the magnificent Philadelphia that has been so universally kind to me. I say it is time we turn around in our city and begin to talk up the things that are in our city, and begin to set them before the world as the people of Chicago, New York, St. Louis, and San Francisco do. Oh, if we only could get that spirit out among our people, that we can do things in Philadelphia and do them well!

Arise, ye millions of Philadelphians, trust in God and man, and believe in the great opportunities that are right here not over in New York or Boston, but here—for business, for everything that is worth living for on earth. There was never an opportunity greater. Let us talk up our own city.

But there are two other young men here to-night, and that is all I will venture to say, because it is too late. One over there gets up and says, "There is going to be a great man in Philadelphia, but never was one." "Oh, is that so? When are you going to be great?" "When I am elected to some political office." Young man, won't you learn a lesson in the primer of politics that it is a prima facie evidence of littleness to hold office under our form of government? Great men get into office sometimes, but what this country needs is men that will do what we tell them to do. This nation—where the people rule—is governed by the people, for the people, and so long as it is, then the office-holder is but the

---

Why do many other cities of the United States get ahead of Philadelphia now? There is only one answer, and that is because our own people talk down their own city.

---

servant of the people, and the Bible says the servant cannot be greater than the master. The Bible says, "He that is sent cannot be greater than Him who sent Him." The people rule, or should rule, and if they do, we do not need the greater men in office. If the great men in America took our offices, we would change to an empire in the next ten years.

I know of a great many young women, now that woman's suffrage is coming, who say, "I am going to be President of the United States some day." I believe in woman's suffrage, and there is no doubt but what it is coming, and I am getting out of the way, anyhow. I may want an office by and by myself; but if the ambition for an office influences the women in their desire to vote, I want to say right here what I say to the young men, that if you only get the privilege of casting one vote, you don't get anything that is worth while. Unless you can control more than one vote, you will be unknown, and your influence so dissipated as practically not to be felt. This country is not run by votes. Do you think it is? It is governed by influence. It is governed by the ambitions and the enterprises which control votes. The young woman that thinks she is going to vote for the sake of holding an office is making an awful blunder.

That other young man gets up and says, "There are going to be great men in this country and in Philadelphia." "Is that so? When?" "When there comes a great war, when we get into difficulty through watchful waiting in Mexico; when we get into war with England over some frivolous deed, or with Japan or China or New Jersey or some distant country. Then I will march up to the cannon's mouth; I will sweep up among the glistening bayonets; I will leap into the arena and tear down the flag and bear it away in triumph. I will come home with stars on my shoulder, and hold every office in the gift of the nation, and I will be great." No, you won't. You think you are going to be made great by an office, but remember that if you are not great before you get the office, you won't be great when you secure it. It will only be a burlesque in that shape.

We had a Peace Jubilee here after the Spanish War. Out West they don't believe this, because they said, "Philadelphia would not have heard of any Spanish War until fifty years hence." Some of you saw the procession go up Broad Street. I was away, but the family wrote to me that the tally-ho coach with Lieutenant Hobson upon it stopped right at the front door and the people shouted, "Hurrah for Hobson!" and if I had been there I would have yelled too, because he deserves much more of his country than he has ever received. But suppose I go into school and say, "Who sunk the *Merrimac* at Santiago?" and if the boys answer me, "Hobson," they will tell me seven-eighths of a lie. There were seven other heroes on that steamer, and they, by virtue of their position, were continually exposed to the Spanish fire, while Hobson, as an officer, might reasonably be behind the smoke-stack. You have gathered in this house your most intelligent people, and yet, perhaps, not one here can name the other seven men.

We ought not to so teach history. We ought to teach that, however humble a man's station may be, if he does his full duty in that place he is just as much entitled to the American people's honor as is the king upon his throne. But we do not so teach. We are now teaching everywhere that the generals do all the fighting.

I remember that, after the war, I went down to see General Robert E. Lee, that magnificent Christian gentleman of whom both North and South are now proud as one of our great Americans. The general told me about his servant, "Rastus," who was an enlisted colored soldier. He called him in one day to make fun of him, and said, "Rastus, I hear that all the rest of your company are killed, and why are you not killed?" Rastus winked at him and said, "Cause when there is any fightin' goin' on I stay back with the generals."

I remember another illustration. I would leave it out but for the fact that when you go to the library to read this lecture, you will find this has been printed in it for twenty-five years. I shut my eyes—shut them close—and lo! I see the faces of my youth. Yes, they sometimes say to me," Your hair is not white; you are working night and day without seeming ever to stop; you can't be old." But when I shut my eyes, like any other man of my years, oh, then come trooping back the faces of the loved and lost of long ago, and I know, whatever men may say, it is evening-time.

I shut my eyes now and look back to my native town in Massachusetts, and I see the cattle-show ground on the mountain-top; I can see the horse-sheds there. I can see the Congregational church; see the town hall and mountaineers' cottages; see a great assembly of people turning out, dressed resplendently, and I can see flags flying and handkerchiefs waving and hear bands playing. I can see that company of soldiers that had re-enlisted marching up on that cattle-show ground. I was but a boy, but I was captain of that company and puffed out with pride. A cambric needle would have burst me all to pieces. Then I thought it was the greatest event that ever came to man on earth. If you have ever thought you would like to be a king or queen, you go and be received by the mayor.

The bands played, and all the people turned out to receive us. I marched up that

CONWELL'S WORLD FAMOUS LECTURE

Common so proud at the head of my troops, and we turned down into the town hall. Then they seated my soldiers down the center aisle and I sat down on the front seat. A great assembly of people a hundred or two—came in to fill the town hall, so that they stood up all around. Then the town officers came in and formed a half-circle. The mayor of the town sat in the middle of the platform. He was a man who had never held office before; but he was a good man, and his friends have told me that I might use this without giving them offense. He was a good man, but he thought an office made a man great. He came up and took his seat, adjusted his powerful spectacles, and looked around, when he suddenly spied me sitting there on the front seat. He came right forward on the platform and invited me up to sit with the town officers. No town officer ever took any notice of me before I went to war, except to advise the teacher to thrash me, and now I was invited up on the stand with the town officers. Oh my! the town mayor was then the emperor, the king of our day and our time. As I came up on the platform they gave me a chair about this far, I would say, from the front.

When I had got seated, the chairman of the Selectmen arose and came forward to the table, and we all supposed he would introduce the Congregational minister, who was the only orator in town, and that he would give the oration to the returning soldiers. But, friends, you should have seen the surprise which ran over the audience when they discovered that the old fellow was going to deliver that speech himself. He had never made a speech in his life, but he fell into the same error that hundreds of other men have fallen into. It seems so strange that a man won't learn he must speak his piece as a boy if he intends to be an orator when he is grown, but he seems to think all he has to do is to hold an office to be a great orator.

So he came up to the front, and brought with him a speech which he had learned by heart walking up and down the pasture, where he had frightened the cattle. He brought the manuscript with him and spread it out on the table so as to be sure he might see it. He adjusted his spectacles and leaned over it for a moment and marched back on that platform, and then came forward like this—tramp, tramp, tramp. He must have studied the subject a great deal, when you come to think of it, because he assumed an "elocutionary" attitude. He rested heavily upon his left heel, threw back his shoulders, slightly advanced the right foot, opened the organs of speech, and advanced his right foot at an angle of forty-five. As he stood in that elocutionary attitude, friends, this is just the way that speech went. Some people say to me, "Don't you exaggerate?" That would be impossible. But I am here for the lesson and not for the story, and this is the way it went:

"Fellow-citizens—" As soon as he heard his voice his fingers began to go like that, his knees began to shake, and then he trembled all over. He choked and swallowed and came around to the table to look at the manuscript. Then he gathered himself up with clenched fists and came back: "Fellow-citizens, we are– Fellow-citizens, we are—we are—we are—we are—we are—we are very happy—we are very happy—we are very happy. We are very happy to welcome back to their native town these soldiers who have fought and bled—and come back again to their native town.—We are especially—we are especially—we are especially. We are especially pleased to see with us to-day this young hero" (that meant me)—" this young hero who in imagination" (friends, remember he said that; if he had not said "in imagination" I would not be egotistic enough to refer to it at all)—" this young hero who in imagination we have seen leading—we have seen leading—leading. We have seen leading his troops on to the deadly breach. We have seen his shining—we have seen his shining—his shining—his shining sword—flashing. Flashing in the sunlight, as he shouted to his troops, 'Come on'!"

Oh dear, dear, dear! how little that good man knew about war. If he had known anything about war at all he ought to have known what any of my G. A. R. comrades here to-night will tell you is true, that it is next to a crime for an officer of infantry ever in time of danger to go ahead of his men. "I, with my shining sword flashing in the sunlight, shouting to my troops, 'Come on'!" I never did it. Do you suppose I would get in front of my men to be shot in front by the enemy and in the back by my own men? That is no place for an officer. The place for the officer in actual battle is behind the line. How often, as a staff officer, I rode down the line, when our men were suddenly called to the line of battle, and the Rebel yells were coming out of the woods, and shouted: "Officers to the rear! Officers to the rear!" Then every officer gets behind the line of private soldiers, and the higher the officer's rank the farther behind he goes. Not because he is any the less

> **Greatness consists not in the holding of some future office, but really consists in doing great deeds with little means and the accomplishment of vast purposes from the private ranks of life. To be great at all one must be great here, now, in Philadelphia.**

brave, but because the laws of war require that. And yet he shouted, "I, with my shining sword—" In that house there sat the company of my soldiers who had carried that boy across the Carolina rivers that he might not wet his feet. Some of them had gone far out to get a pig or a chicken. Some of them had gone to death under the shell-swept pines in the mountains of Tennessee, yet in the good man's speech they were scarcely known. He did refer to them, but only incidentally. The hero of the hour was this boy. Did the nation owe him anything? No, nothing then and nothing now. Why was he the hero? Simply because that man fell into that same human error—that this boy was great because he was an officer and these were only private soldiers.

Oh, I learned the lesson then that I will never forget so long as the tongue of the bell of time continues to swing for me. Greatness consists not in the holding of some future office, but really consists in doing great deeds with little means and the accomplishment of vast purposes from the private ranks of life. To be great at all one must be great here, now, in Philadelphia. He who can give to this city better streets and better sidewalks, better schools and more colleges, more happiness and more civilization, more of God, he will be great anywhere. Let every man or woman here, if you never hear me again, remember this, that if you wish to be great at all, you must begin where you are and what you are, in Philadelphia, now. He that can give to his city any blessing, he who can be a good citizen while he lives here, he that can make better homes, he that can be a blessing whether he works in the shop or sits behind the counter or keeps house, whatever be his life, he who would be great anywhere must first be great in his own Philadelphia.

APPENDIX

Since certain principles found in chapters 7 and 8 will be useful to the reader, they are summarized in this appendix for the purpose of assisting the reader in practical application. As these principles are read and reflected upon, they can inspire individuals to take appropriate action steps to achieve purposeful goals with noble motives.

PRICELESS DIAMOND NUGGETS FROM CHAPTER SEVEN
How Russell Conwell Started Temple University from Nothing

1. Conwell believed that if enough people need what you have to offer, you can become wealthy or "well-off" by simply fulfilling that need—it is entirely an automatic process.

2. He also believed that if a need is legitimate and justifiable, the very need itself carries the inherent and potential power to supply the answer for the need.

3. If you truly work at fulfilling a need, you usually will not get rich quickly. In fact, your motives will often be tested as to whether or not you are in it for the right reasons. Temple University was not a profitable venture for Conwell during the first several years. It was basically like doing charity work, but it paid off greatly after many years of sacrifice and challenge. If Conwell would have started the university just with the motive of getting rich, he would have quit before things really got off the ground, but he had a passion for purpose that kept him going when many others would have quit.

4. Conwell was driven by his desire to help others to help themselves. Money was not his primary motivation—meeting the needs of people was.

5. Conwell was not a minister who merely preached to people. He always sought practical ways to put his faith into action by helping others.

6. Conwell did not seek fame, riches, or glory for himself. His number-one driving force was "to always do good in the Master's name," and he also thrived on giving others their due credit.

7. Conwell did not want a university only for the privileged; he was concerned about the common, working-class citizen and the poor as well as the rich. He was a champion of the oppressed and the underprivileged, and this was

one of the keys to his success. "He that hath pity upon the poor lendeth unto the LORD; and that which he hath given will he pay him again" (Proverbs 19:17).

8. Though he saw the need to feed the hungry, Conwell discovered that he could help a lot more people through proper instruction than through the mere handout of material goods or food.

PRICELESS DIAMOND NUGGETS FROM CHAPTER EIGHT
The Hospitals Russell Conwell Started and Managed

1. Conwell believed that if you have a pure motive to help others and you start with what you've got, God can then turn that into a lot.

2. He also believed that giving someone a helping hand does not necessarily mean you should give him a handout, and giving someone the wrong type of help can actually cripple him for life.

3. Conwell was a practical leader who made changes to accommodate the needs of the people when it was in his power to do so.

4. Because Conwell had an eternal perspective concerning the well-being of the souls of men and women, the Lord blessed his efforts all the more.

5. Conwell was a master at maximizing his time and energy.

6. Conwell proved the simple fact that starting something purposeful, developing a team of players with a plan, and simply sticking to the plan is a key to success—but nothing happens if you never get started because you are waiting for the grandiose scheme or "big beginning."

7. Where the spirit of life is, something must grow!

INDEX

INDEX

NOTES

NOTES

NOTES

NOTES

NOTES

NOTES

NOTES

NOTES